the better **people** leader

the
better
people
leader

Charles A. Coonradt

with Lisa Ann Thomson

GIBBS SMITH
TO ENRICH AND INSPIRE HUMANKIND

To Carla—my wife, companion, and
business partner since 1975—and my family.
They are the better people who inspire
and motivate me.

© 2012 Gibbs Smith, Publisher

© 2007 Charles A. Coonradt

Published by
Gibbs Smith, Publisher
P.O. Box 667
Layton, Utah 84041

Orders: 1.800.835.4993
www.gibbs-smith.com

Designed by Jody Billert / Design Literate, Inc.
Printed and bound in the U.S.A.

Library of Congress Cataloging-in-Publication Data
Coonradt, Charles A.
 The better people leader / Charles A. Coonradt with Lisa Ann Thomson. — 1st ed.
 p. cm.
 ISBN-13: 978-1-4236-3086-9 (paperback)
 ISBN-13: 978-1-4236-0158-6 (hardcover)
 1. Leadership—Study and teaching. I. Thomson, Lisa Ann. II. Title.

HD57.7C667 2007
658.4'092—dc22

 2007009188

Contents

Foreword

As the head football coach of the University of Florida Gators, I experienced the honor of heading a team that was led to greatness by twenty-two seniors. I was hired by the University of Florida in 2004 to lead the football program to its expected high level of excellence. After two years at Florida, I found and helped cultivate the team leaders that would inspire the team to the 2006 BCS National Championship.

So I know what it means to lead teams to even greater performance levels or championship caliber. Early on in my coaching career, I had the honor and privilege of working for some "better people leaders," amazing coaches who I came to regard as my personal mentors. These men didn't just do the minimum. They didn't just get by. No, they wholeheartedly invested themselves in the success of the team and of each individual player and staff member. They showed

me what it meant to go much further—and as a result, I learned what I had to do in order to win: develop leaders.

I started my coaching career as a graduate assistant for Coach Earle Bruce at Ohio State University. Coach Bruce knew everything about everyone on the team and staff and nothing escaped his eye. His attention to detail was astounding and he was always prepared for anything that happened to arise. He demanded that his players attend class and work hard academically and on the practice field. If a coach did not coach to his standards, he coached that person as well as the players. Coach Bruce invited me to join him at Colorado State University as the receivers' coach and the program quickly started to improve under his guidance. After the first season, CSU was invited to the Freedom Bowl and defeated Oregon. It was CSU's first bowl appearance in almost fifty years.

When Coach Sonny Lubick took over the helm at CSU, I was invited to remain as the receivers' coach. Success continued under Coach Lubick. While their styles were different, Coach Bruce and Coach Lubick were extraordinarily similar in meticulous preparation, hard work, and knowledge of every player in the program.

At the University of Notre Dame, I was the receivers' coach under head coach Lou Holtz. In addition to learning more about preparation and hard work, I was able to learn from an outstanding motivator who knew exactly what to say and when to say certain things to drive and inspire his teams.

What I learned from all three of these mentors was that people—both the players and the coaching staff—are a coach's most important resource. I learned that the more you invest in your people and the more you do to develop their leadership skills, the more you gain from them. For me that means investing the time and effort to recruit the best. It means getting to know each and every player on the team, including each person's strengths and weaknesses, so that I

can make sure his talents are being used to the full potential. It means knowing what best motivates my players and what needs they have that must be met in order to get the best effort out of them. Most importantly, getting to know your team members shows them that you truly care about them, about their success, and about the success of the team. And the more you care, the more your players care about doing the best they can for you and leading others to do likewise.

In this powerful, insightful leadership book, Chuck Coonradt teaches you the fundamental lesson that every leader needs to know—that every leader has the power to lead a team that was just getting by to extraordinary accomplishments. This book will show you exactly what it takes to do that. It's not easy—it takes lots of commitment and hard work. But it's far from impossible. On the contrary, it's extremely possible for anyone who is willing to invest the time and effort to understand and apply the principles that Chuck outlines so well in this book.

Here is a book that finally articulates the secret to the success of the world's better people leaders: the fact that in order to experience success, you have to first create an environment for success to happen in. It's something I do every day as the coach of national champions, and if you do it too, you will lead your team to greatness.

Urban Meyer
Former Head Football Coach, University of Florida

Acknowledgments

To Lisa Thomson for unmangling this manuscript, challenging me on the parts that didn't make sense, and making sense of it all.

To the leaders at Gibbs Smith, Publisher, Gibbs and Christopher, who experienced our work and had the foresight to see a book in that work.

To Lisa Anderson for her clear-sightedness as our editor, who made this work so pleasant for you, the reader.

To all the team members of the Game of Work, who labor tirelessly bringing our message to thousands of participants each year, and through whose efforts so many of the stories of better people leaders are gained.

Most of all, to Carla Coonradt, my incredible alter ego (she clearly deserves co-author status), who sees the needed "fills" and makes what we do better.

Introduction

What is it that we love about certain movies? Think about *Miracle,* which is based on the story of the 1980 U.S. Hockey Team and their dramatic Olympic gold medal victory. *Remember the Titans* is the story of a newly integrated high school and its football team in 1971 as they overcome prejudice among themselves and the community to achieve an undefeated season. What about *We Are Marshall* and its telling of a young coach determined to rebuild the football program at Marshall University after seventy-five members of its football team and coaching staff were killed in a plane crash in 1970? Who doesn't feel inspired by these stories, particularly knowing they are based on real events and real people? Even fictional characters like Akeelah, her teacher, and her principal in *Akeelah and the Bee* make us cheer as we watch this young girl rise above her circumstances to excel and win the National Spelling Bee. And one of my favorites is *The Mighty Ducks*—the tale of a ragtag group of

teen hockey players and their unlikely coach who turn a losing team into a championship team.

We love to see average people do above-average things. We love to see people change their minds and hearts and reach a new level of understanding. We especially love to see inspirational leaders motivate others to reach new levels of greatness. And whether the characters are real or fictional, the underlying principles are true: average people can do above-average things; people can change their minds and hearts; and great leaders inspire people to greatness every day.

I see it happen in businesses regularly. In my work as a management consultant, I have taught many principles of leadership, and I have been thrilled as I've seen people take these principles to incredible levels, far beyond my own expectations. I love to see teams and their coaches come from behind and win.

One such team I know was led by Don Pritchard. Don was hired at a manufacturing company to manage inventory, shipping, and receiving. His department was responsible for warehousing inventory and fulfilling requests to supply materials for other departments. Don had almost twenty years of experience in manufacturing, but he had never managed a warehouse before. To make the situation more challenging, the department was suffering from an extremely bad reputation in the company. This department experienced only ninety percent accuracy when a request came in, meaning one in ten items was not on the shelf when they went looking for it, and therefore, one in ten requests could not be fulfilled. That caused tremendous frustration for the workers within the department and for others outside the department who relied on the warehouse stores. The department was widely criticized by the rest of the company, and they were blamed—rightly or wrongly—for a variety of problems. Morale within the department was terrible. "I think if I were to put it in one phrase, they lacked self-esteem as a group," Don told me.

Don's challenge from the company was to improve the way this department functioned. Now, many managers might come into a situation like this and clean house. If they fire everyone who has been causing this mess for so long, they can get new bodies and train them how they want them to work. But Don took a different approach. He didn't clean house. He remodeled.

Don decided he needed to get to know each person on his team individually. He wanted to learn their strengths and their weaknesses and hear their frustrations. He took the time not just to interview each person but also to work alongside each of his employees. By spending the time to work with each individual (and, Don assures me, it does take an investment of time), he learned a lot about the business, the department, the problems, and the people on his team. He also discovered many of the reasons why the system was not functioning well. He began to understand why it was taking ten minutes to fulfill one order and why one in ten times the item was not on the shelf when someone went looking for it.

But perhaps more importantly, by learning about the department from the employees themselves, Don empowered them to help solve the problems. He was able to say to people, "That's an interesting problem. What would you do to solve it?" Through the process, he learned individual strengths and weaknesses and was able to better utilize his people. "I don't think there's anyone who comes to work and wants to do a bad job," Don says. "Just play to their strengths. Don't put them in a position where they will fail."

In the end, his department, as a team, developed a new system of organization. They reorganized the warehouse, they improved their processes, and they let go of inefficiencies. As a result, accuracy went from ninety percent to more than ninety-nine percent. In reorganizing the warehouse they saved warehouse space by thirty-five percent. And with the same number of people on

staff they were able to accomplish ten to fifteen percent more work each day.

Don didn't wish for better people. Don coached who he had. As a result, his department changed dramatically. Everyone in the department was formally recognized and commended by the company for the significant improvements he or she had made. You can imagine what that did for morale.

This is the power of a good leader. It's not just about making the department work better. It's about making the *people* work better and feel proud of their accomplishments. Because people do want to feel proud of their accomplishments. Like Don said, nobody comes to work wanting to lose. They want to win.

I founded my business, The Game of Work, on the belief that if you apply the principles of sports and recreation to the workplace, you can create a sense of motivation, urgency, and, yes, even fun in your company that will translate into better productivity, happier employees, and a more successful business.

I've observed over the years that people will pay for the privilege of working harder than they will work when they are paid. It's a mouthful, I know, but follow me on this one. I see it all the time. I live in a ski town in the Rocky Mountains and I see people collectively spend thousands and thousands of dollars every day during the winter to spend hours and hours freezing, falling, and flying down the mountain until they can hardly catch their breath. I've seen people spend hundreds, even thousands, of dollars on backpacking gear so they can walk for fifteen miles a day for a week, sleep on the ground every night, cook freeze-dried food over a fire, and battle bugs, rodents, reptiles, and sunburns. I've seen people pay to jump out of airplanes, climb mountains, backpack through Europe, and drive cattle at a dude ranch. In short, I've seen people pay an awful lot of money to work awfully hard.

I've also seen people call their union rep if they didn't get an afternoon break. I've seen people absolutely refuse to come in a minute early or stay a minute late. I've seen people spend hours writing e-mails for every reason except work. I've seen people spend hours "tidying" their desk and watching the clock. One of my favorites was a receptionist who rolled her eyes and told the person on her cell phone to "hang on" while she grabbed the company's main line—like it was an interruption.

People will pay money to work their tails off, yet they will not work their tails off when they are being paid money. I'm not suggesting all American workers are lazy. There are a lot of hard workers out there getting it done every day. I am suggesting there are principles that motivate people to work hard when they are recreating and those principles can be successfully applied to the workplace.

I'll say it again—everybody wants to win. Yet millions of workers go to work every day and do their jobs without knowing how to win—without knowing their goals, without knowing if they are progressing toward those goals or even how progress is measured, without knowing the rules, and ultimately without bringing their best productivity to the company. Unless people believe winning is possible, they will never exert the kind of effort it would take to win. They won't exert even half that effort. When that happens, nobody wins.

I don't blame the workers. I actually blame the coaches. Oh sure, there are workers who don't work and won't work no matter how ideal an environment they are in. Let those guys work for your competition. There are lots of people who work hard. They give you their all and would give you more if they knew how. As a coach, you can have incredible talent on your team, but if you don't create an environment for success, your team will never be incredible. And without incredible teams, companies don't become incredible. They plod along at best and falter at worst.

So I'm going to focus on the coaches from here on out—or as I like to call them: better people leaders. In this book's companion volume, *The Game of Work,* I expound more thoroughly on how the principles that lead to motivation in recreation can lead to motivation—and remarkable success—in the workplace. But because people are central to any success (and any failure) in a company, the concepts of becoming a great coach and coaching your people to greatness merit special treatment.

Better people leaders motivate, inspire, empower, and lead their teams to greatness—greatness their teams often didn't know they had in them. How that is done will fill the rest of this book. I have observed and coached and worked alongside thousands of leaders in my career. Over that time, certain themes have come up continually in the best of the leaders I have worked with. I have compiled those themes in this book in hopes of helping others become the kind of leaders who inspire, like Don Pritchard and others do. But I'll warn you up front: I believe in fundamentals. I hope as you read you say again and again, "Yes, of course!" because you knew it all along. These are fundamentals that can be applied at work, at home, and even at play that will help you get the most from whatever team you are called to lead.

·one·

People Make the Difference

"Some people say it is wrong to regard life as a game; I don't think so. . . . Life to me means the greatest of all games. The danger lies in treating it as a trivial game, a game to be taken lightly, and a game in which the rules don't matter much. . . . The game has to be played fairly, or it is no game at all. And even to win the game is not the chief end. The chief end is to win it honorably and splendidly."
SIR ERNEST SHACKLETON[1]

It is often called the Heroic Age of Polar Exploration. The early days of the twentieth century are punctuated with grand and dramatic adventures as explorers from England, Scotland, Sweden, Japan, and elsewhere headed north and south to reach the literal ends of the

earth. The United States claimed the North Pole in 1909.[2] Norway claimed the South Pole in 1911.[3]

Sir Ernest Shackleton had twice been on expeditions hoping to be the first to reach the South Pole, but twice the expeditions failed to reach their goal. With the Pole claimed by the Norwegians, Shackleton set out on a third expedition—to be the first to traverse the Antarctic continent. "It is the last great Polar journey that can be made," he wrote in the expedition's prospectus. "It will be a greater journey than the journey to the Pole and back."[4]

Despite not reaching their goals, Shackleton's previous Antarctic sojourns had made him a national hero in England. When it was time to man his ship for the Imperial Trans-Antarctic Expedition, he was flooded with requests from nearly five thousand would-be explorers. Shackleton took few things more seriously in preparing for his expedition than assembling the people who would accompany him, despite what some might call unorthodox interviewing practices. He hired meteorologist and banjo player Leonard Hussey because he "thought [he] looked funny," he later confessed. He then explained, "Loyalty comes easier to a cheerful person than to one who carries a heavy countenance."[5]

Crew member Reginald W. James, who was hired as a physicist, recalled being asked not as much about his science skills as about his teeth and voice: "Shackleton asked me if my teeth were good, if I suffered from varicose veins, if my circulation was good, if I had a good temper, and if I could sing. At this question, I probably looked a bit taken back, for I remember he said, 'Oh, I don't mean any Caruso stuff; but I suppose you can shout a bit with the boys?'"[6]

Artist George Marston was hired for an earlier Shackleton expedition after he was the only one of three candidates who made haste—in the rain from Cornwall to London—to arrive on short notice for an interview. "I promptly engaged him," Shackleton said.

"I thought that if a man could be as quick as that in order to get a position, he was the man for it; and, as it turned out, my opinion was more than justified." So justified that Shackleton hired him again for the trans-Antarctic journey.[7]

He brought on Tom Crean and Frank Wild, both of whom had excellent Antarctic experience and both of whom Shackleton had worked with before. He knew the strengths they would bring to the team: Crean's good head and stout heart had been demonstrated in a heroic dash to save his companions on another expedition, and Wild's leadership had been key to Shackleton at crucial and even desperate moments during a previous bid for the South Pole.[8]

The *Endurance* set sail for Antarctica on August 8, 1914, and Shackleton tinkered with the staff to the very last. Four men who left England on the *Endurance* were let off in Buenos Aires, Argentina, and a young stowaway who had joined them there was kept on.[9] Shackleton hand-selected every man who was to embark on the Imperial Trans-Antarctic Expedition aboard the ship *Endurance*. He learned not only if they could sail a ship or study the weather, but also if they could sing or tell a joke. He sought to hire character and attitude as much as skill and experience. As history would tell, it would be these men who would mean the difference between success and failure—even as the goal changed from crossing the continent to surviving its ocean.

The plan had been to sail the *Endurance* to a drop-off point on the continent. A team would winter there while the ship and crew returned to Buenos Aires. In the spring the land team would traverse the continent, ending at the Ross Sea coast where they would be picked up.[10] However, before they left Buenos Aires, reports warned of unusually severe ice conditions. The reports were confirmed at a whaling station on South Georgia Island—some were calling it the

worst ice conditions in living memory—and it was suggested they postpone their journey until the next season.[11]

Shackleton did not postpone the journey. The *Endurance* left South Georgia Island on December 5, 1914, and hit ice pack only two days later. For more than a month the ship and its crew toiled among the ice floes until the unthinkable happened. There were no more lanes through which the ship could slip. The ice shifted and gathered until the *Endurance* was completely engulfed. She was trapped in the ice.[12]

Shackleton declared the marooned ship a winter station, with all twenty-eight men—and dozens of dogs and a cat—still aboard. "Shackleton at this time showed one of his sparks of real greatness," wrote Alexander Macklin, one of the ship's two surgeons. "He did not rage at all, or show outwardly the slightest sign of disappointment; he told us simply and calmly that we must winter in the pack, explained its dangers and possibilities; never lost his optimism, and prepared for winter."[13]

Shackleton's greatness, as well as that of his men, would spark throughout the coming ordeal. From the able hand of the ship's carpenter to the creative concoctions of the ship's cook to the sharp eye of the expedition's photographer, each member of the team had a part to play and was expected to play it wholeheartedly. Assignments were made to log the stores, exercise the dogs, scrub the floors, melt the ice, and skin the penguins. Slideshows, sing-alongs, readings, and even soccer games and dog sledge competitions were organized.[14] Their situation was precarious, but spirits remained high. "We are now six months out from England and during the whole of this time we have all pulled well together and with almost complete lack of friction. A more agreeable set of gentlemen and good fellows one could not wish for shipmates," wrote the ship's captain, Frank Worsley, in his diary. "We seem to be a wonderful happy family but

I think Sir Ernest is the real secret of our unanimity," echoed Thomas Orde-Lees, the expedition's ski expert and motor sledge operator. [15]

The crew spent ten long months aboard their trapped ship. Then in October 1915, the unforgiving ice completed its task, shifting until it slowly and cruelly crushed the ship. On October 27, 1915, the men abandoned ship with nowhere to go but an ice floe in the middle of the Weddell Sea. [16]

They lived on the ice for five months. Then almost all of a sudden the melting and cracking floes forced the group to make a hasty and dangerous dash for land in three small lifeboats. In the most dangerous and terrifying leg of their journey so far, they reached Elephant Island after seven days at sea and found the land as inhospitable as the icy water. Shackleton immediately decided their only chance for survival was to make another dangerous crossing in the open ocean to South Georgia Island, some eight hundred miles away. Five were selected to accompany Shackleton, and the others stayed behind. [17] "The men ashore formed a pathetic group," noted Captain Worsley, who was aboard the small *James Caird* as it sailed out of the harbor at Elephant Island. "As long as they thought that we could see them they kept up a wonderful appearance of optimism and heartiness." [18]

The six men were on the ocean for seventeen days. They endured bitter cold, scanty rations, intense seasickness, and a hurricane that they later learned sunk a five-hundred-ton steamer in the same waters. But they reached South Georgia Island. [19] They landed on the side opposite the manned whaling stations and were faced with a final challenge: to cross the uncharted mountains that lay between them and the stations. Shackleton, Crean, and Worsley made the overland crossing, leaving the other three with the battered *James Caird.* It was an exhausting thirty-six hours during which they hardly stopped. When they reached Stromness Station, they were

unrecognizable in their desperate condition. They were taken to the manager of the station, a man Shackleton knew. An old Norwegian whaler recorded the moment in broken English: "Manager say: 'Who the hell are you?' and terrible bearded man in the centre of the three say very quietly: 'My name is Shackleton.' Me—I turn away and weep."[20]

Throughout the ordeal, it was demonstrated again and again that Shackleton knew his men and had chosen wisely. The "funny" meteorologist and banjo player proved a gift during the boredom and fear of many months trapped by the ice. The crusty carpenter worked miracles with scraps from the *Endurance* wreckage to shore up the tiny lifeboats for a journey through icy seas and open ocean. The captain was a gifted navigator who saw them through eight hundred miles of open ocean to South Georgia Island with only glimpses of the sun and stars and waterlogged maps. Shackleton's second in command, left with the men on Elephant Island awaiting rescue, proved a leader in every right and saw their men through the darkest hour of the ordeal. Shackleton himself had demanded and given loyalty, optimism, and every ounce of his strength for the survival of the group.[21] The people had made the difference.

On August 30, 1916, more than two years after setting off for a trans-Antarctic land crossing, a small ship appeared in the bay of Elephant Island. Shackleton's men were rescued. A quick letter to his wife summarized the event. "I have done it. . . . Not a life lost and we have been through hell."[22]

THE RIGHT PEOPLE

Sir Ernest Shackleton and his team are proof that any endeavor lives and dies by its people. Another group of people with a different leader may have had a very different outcome. In fact, other Antarctic expeditions did have very different outcomes. Another epic

hero of the Antarctic age and a contemporary of Shackleton, Captain Robert Falcon Scott, also found himself and his team in the harshest of circumstances after a failed bid for the South Pole in 1912. Scott and his team reached the Pole only to find the Norwegian flag flying over it. As the disappointed men made the eight-hundred-mile land journey back to their ship, one by one they died. The last three were found the following spring, Scott among them, frozen to death in their tent. [23]

The point is not to minimize Scott's heroic efforts. But it provides an interesting contrast. One group of people facing failure, disappointment, and the most trying of conditions may handle its circumstances very differently than another group of people in similar circumstances. Many have debated whether Shackleton himself showed lack of judgment or tunnel vision when he chose to proceed despite warnings about the ice from as far away as Argentina. Perhaps he did. But the reality remains the same: when the decision was made to move forward and the expedition proceeded, he was there with the right people.

Shackleton had used his previous experience and his knowledge of Antarctic exploration to seek out the right people for his expedition. He knew what the right people looked like. "The men selected must be qualified for the work, and they must also have the special qualifications required to meet polar conditions," Shackleton noted. "They must be able to live together in harmony for a long period of time without outside communication, and it must be remembered that the men whose desires lead them to the untrodden paths of the world have generally marked individuality. It was no easy matter for me to select the staff." [24]

When the team faced challenges that appeared insurmountable, everyone rose to his highest level of performance to meet those challenges. The fact that not a life was lost was due as much to the

right people as it was to the leader who knew enough to assemble them.

GETTING IT RIGHT IN BUSINESS

The success or failure of any business—no matter the market, technology, money, or strategy—also comes down to the people involved in it. Why is it that the Ritz-Carlton can command hundreds, even thousands, of dollars a night for a hotel stay when Holiday Inn offers the same basic product: a private room and bath, a bed with clean sheets, and cable? What's the difference between spending a day skiing Aspen or a day skiing nearby Breckenridge when they're both in the Colorado Rockies and it's the same basic activity? Why did the Boston Celtics dominate the 1960s in basketball but not the 1970s, or why did the Chicago Bulls dominate the 1990s and not the 2000s? Why is shopping at Nordstrom different than shopping at the Gap? It's the people.

But as Jim Collins points out in *Good to Great,* "People are *not* your most important asset. The *right* people are."[25] No doubt you can think of experiences when the success of a project hinged on a person at your office. Was the project ultimately successful because you had the right person who stepped up and excelled in a pinch? Or was the project a debacle because the person couldn't handle the pressure, didn't have the skills, or wasn't motivated to perform? The difference between where your organization is today and where you'd like it to be is the people. You might have heard the longstanding GE slogan, "Progress is our most important product." I would qualify that sentiment with a slogan of my own: "You don't make progress without the right people." Getting, training, and keeping the right people needs to be at the core of any successful business strategy. A strategy isn't worth the paper it's printed on if it isn't executed. And who will execute? The people.

That puts tremendous responsibility on the manager of those people. Whether you are the CEO of a multinational corporation or you have a staff of hundreds under your direction or you've been assigned to keep the intern busy, as a leader of people you wield the power to enable and ennoble those you manage. You also wield the ability to demoralize and crush them. *How* you wield that power will appear not only in the faces of those you lead but in every financial, sales, inventory, and miscellaneous report that lands on your desk. The way your employees feel about the company will be reflected in everything they do. And the way employees feel about a company is primarily determined by the way they feel about their boss.

So for the boss, it's about unlocking the potential in each person on the team. It's a belief in the expandability, not expendability, of people. It's trusting that people will rise to the challenge of their responsibilities as they are led responsibly and reasonably.

In the coming chapters we'll look at what it takes to be the boss, coach, and leader who enables and ennobles your team, and I'll share some fundamentals of people leadership that I've seen work magic in businesses. Sir Ernest Shackleton demonstrated in a dramatic way what good leadership and the right people can accomplish. But you can see it every day—even in ways that are as personally dramatic to you—as you become a better leader of people.

THE HEART OF THE MATTER

As Sir Ernest Shackleton and his crew demonstrated, the success or failure of any enterprise comes down to the people involved in it. Getting, training, and keeping the right people needs to be at the core of any successful business strategy. The manager of those people must

- focus on unlocking the potential in each person on the team;
- believe in the expandability, not expendability, of people;
- and trust that people will rise to the challenge of their responsibilities as they are led responsibly and reasonably.

·two·

The Better People Leader

The first step to becoming a better leader of people is knowing what one looks like. I often use the term "coach" in my work not just because it fits with the whole philosophy of the Game of Work, but also because I believe that for managers and executives, or even parents and spouses, "coaching" is a better description of what we do, or should be doing, than just about anything else.

But recently I've found myself using slightly different terminology. I've taken to calling coaches "better people leaders." Lots of people lead people. But some are better people leaders than others. What makes them better? What sets a better people leader apart from an average people leader? It begins with a leader's attributes and ends with the execution of those attributes in leadership situations.

So we start with the attributes. This is a list of what I have observed over the years in better people leaders. As I take you

through these attributes, think of yourself and do a little self inspection. I even hope you squirm a little. Honestly assess yourself against the attributes of better people leaders—even if it means you have to admit your weak points as well as your strong points. I'll ask some self assessment questions at the end to help you gauge your current standing and then offer tips for improvement.

They have a global vision.

They see the big picture, they think outside the box, they don't have tunnel vision—use whatever cliché you want, but the fundamental remains the same: the better people leader has a bigger view of her world. She sees where she is heading, where she currently is en route, and what's around her. You can compare her to the architect who sees the final skyscraper before it's articulated on paper, to the composer who hears the whole symphony before he scribbles out a note, to the artist who envisions the finished work and knows just where to paint the first stroke.

Or you can compare her to the CEO who knows where her company is today and where it should be next month, next year, in five years, in ten years. She also knows where her competition is and where the market is, and she watches closely to see where they both are heading. She knows the skills and talents of her people today and what they can be in the future. She doesn't just plug away at today's questions or even tomorrow's, but she thinks, plans, and prepares for the long run.

They can break down the global vision into steps.

The beauty of the better people leader is that he doesn't lose his head in the realms of global visions. He also has his feet firmly planted on the ground and can determine—and communicate—the sequence of steps that will achieve the vision.

ATTRIBUTES OF BETTER PEOPLE LEADERS

They have a global vision.

They can break down the global vision into steps.

They focus on team excellence rather than their ego.

They know their team members.

They care about their team members.

They know their stuff.

They have great confidence in their players.

They coach their players where they need it.

They know when to cheer and when to challenge.

They are patient, persistent, prodding.

They minimize uncertainty.

They are consistent.

Perhaps most importantly, the better people leader knows the *next best step* to attaining the global vision—by month, by player, by account, by behavior, by whatever digestible chunk it might be. He has the ability to link the details to the vision. You might say he has a micro understanding of the macro and can determine the next best step for reaching his larger goals.

For example, I knew of a printing company that had a great reputation with its current clientele but wanted to significantly expand its client base and revenue. However, the company had older equipment and hadn't kept abreast of changes in printing technolo-

gy. The owner wanted to see the company grow, but he failed to acknowledge that printing technologies had changed and his competition had changed with them. Until the company identified and then took the next best step—upgrading its equipment—it could no longer offer competitive services because of its dated technology. The company finally did and it continues to thrive as a regional printer.

They focus on team excellence rather than their ego.

When it came time to take the 2006 USA Basketball Team's official photo, the new head coach and managing director were positioned right in the middle. But that's not where they stayed. "We aren't going to sit there. Coaches will be on the side," said Mike Krzyzewski, coach of team USA and Duke University's men's basketball team. "The players are the most important, and they are supported by us. The only way to accomplish what we want to accomplish is to do it together. It's not about me or any single individual."[1]

The better people leader supplants his need for a personal win with the need for a team win. He seeks to develop the potential of the team, motivate them to victory, and then let them take the credit. Through the research that became *Good to Great*, Jim Collins found that superstar (read: super ego) CEOs rarely led "great" companies. They often led "good" companies. The great companies were more often led by CEOs with very different characteristics: modesty, self-effacement, and humility. They were also fanatically driven to achieve company, rather than personal, success.[2]

Shackleton could have let his ego get in the way when his ship became trapped in the ice and the expedition came to a halt. He could have let himself become despondent and miserable at this failure; instead, he turned his focus to the team and to leading them through the winter.

The better people leader is always focused on the growth and success of the people on his team. If the consequence is that he gets squeezed out the top because he's trained people on his team to be better at his job than he is, then good for him. He's probably onto something better himself.

Charles Percy is a great example of this. He was a business leader and a former senator for Illinois. In 1949 he was made CEO of Bell & Howell Corporation—at just twenty-nine years old.[3] A national business newspaper interviewed him shortly after he was named president, and the conversation went something like this:

Reporter: "How did you make this incredible jump in such a short time?"

Percy: "I read the book."

Reporter: "What do you mean?"

Percy: "When I got my first position at Bell and Howell, I applied the standard time-management principles:

1. Itemize. I listed the results I wanted and the tasks required to achieve them.
2. Categorize. I put similar items together.
3. Prioritize. I decided what things were most important and which ones could be put aside for later.
4. Delegate or eliminate. I decided on what could better be done by someone else and, more important, what didn't have to be done at all."

Reporter: "What's so unusual about that?"

Percy: "Some might find it unusual that I delegated or eliminated everything."

Reporter: "Everything? Weren't you worried about having nothing to do?"

Percy: "No, not for long."

Reporter: "What happened?"

Percy: "Interestingly enough, another position opened up in the department. When the personnel manager called down for the specifications to begin the hiring search, my manager said, 'We don't need to hire anyone. Let's just give the job to Percy. He doesn't have anything to do.'"

Reporter: "What did you do then?"

Percy: "The same thing I did before: I itemized, categorized, prioritized, and delegated or eliminated."

Reporter: "How much of your work did you delegate or eliminate this time?"

Percy: "All of it."

Reporter: "Didn't that worry you?"

Percy: "Not really. Before long the department manager's position became available. When the personnel manager called down for the position specifications, the boss said, 'We don't need to hire anybody. We'll just give the job to Percy. He doesn't have anything to do.' This went on for some time, until, five years later, the board of directors was looking for a new chief executive officer. Guess what they said: 'Let's give the job to Percy. He doesn't have anything to do.'"[4]

Under Charles Percy's leadership, company sales grew thirty-two-fold, employment grew twelve-fold, and the company went public.[5]

They know their team members.

Knowing the individuals on your team is more than just knowing their names and knowing what projects they are working on. Knowing their names is a great start, and knowing their projects is even better. But what else do you know about them? Do you know their husband's or wife's name? Do they have kids? What are their names? What do they do when they aren't at work? Did you know Bob runs marathons and Annie loves to water ski? Do they have a

particular talent or hobby you could tap for the next company party? Are there situations at home you ought to be aware of?

I was discussing this point at a workshop, and someone mentioned an Army squad leader he knew. The leader kept a book full of information about every member of the squad—if they were married, if they had kids, what their back stories were, etc. His rationale for keeping such a record was simple: one of the best ways to keep his soldiers safe was to know them. If he knew his soldiers and did everything he could to keep them happy, then those soldiers would give him everything they had. If those soldiers were worried about their families or had other things occupying their minds that he didn't know about, then he couldn't do anything to help. And that didn't help the individual or the team.

They care about their team members.

To know your team is to be concerned for them. You've heard the saying, "I don't care how much you know until I know how much you care." Better people leaders genuinely care about their employees, and their employees feel their sincere concern. They care about employees' successes on the job, and they care about their happiness off the job. It may be something as simple as recognizing a contribution and saying, "Thank you for your hard work." Or it may be something as dramatic as helping during a family emergency.

I love the story told in Ken Follet's *On Wings of Eagles*. It recounts a dramatic rescue mission undertaken by Ross Perot, founder of Electronic Data Systems Corporation and chairman at the time. During the Middle East hostage crisis, he set out to free two of his employees from an Iranian prison and safely evacuate dozens of Americans. The main story itself is a dramatic example of a leader showing his employees how much he cares by orchestrating a rescue mission even the U.S. military couldn't do. But there is an anecdote

within the bigger story that exemplifies on a very personal level how a better people leader cares about his employees on and off the job.

Jay Coburn, who was a key player in the rescue operation, relates an experience when his son was born. The baby appeared to be healthy, but the day after his birth, doctors detected a heart abnormality. Coburn and his wife were beside themselves. Coburn called his boss to tell him of the problems, and his boss put him on hold. When he came back on the line, he had Ross Perot with him. Coburn was a low-level employee in a different state; he was shocked that the founder and chairman was on the phone. In the course of a short conversation, Perot got a leading cardiac surgeon on the line who was in turn able to get the child immediately transferred to a larger hospital with top specialists. In the end, the child's problems were addressed and he went on to thrive. For Coburn, the experience left a lasting impression about what the chairman of his company was willing to do for his employees.[6]

Whether it's a dramatic display of concern such as this or a simple acknowledgement of a tough day, the better people leader demonstrates to his employees how much he cares by his actions as well as his words.

They know their stuff.

Once they know how much you care, they actually do care how much you know. People generally have little patience for bosses who they consider less than competent. Can I invoke *Dilbert* here? Have you ever read a *Dilbert* cartoon and thought, "Hmmm. I wonder if Scott Adams knows someone at my company." *Dilbert* is popular because far too many workers can relate, particularly to the Pointy-Haired Boss and the frustration of his staff. The Pointy-Haired Boss is depicted as a manager who knows nothing about anything, really, and least of all about the business he manages. *Dilbert*

wouldn't be funny if the Pointy-Haired Boss were intelligent, informed, and understood his business. The better people leader isn't funny.

One of my favorite better people leaders is Bob Wheaton, president and general manager of Deer Valley Ski Resort in Utah. Each winter, the Game of Work hosts a coaches' ski retreat at Deer Valley, and Bob gives us a tour of the facilities. I've been on the tour dozens of times, but I am continually amazed at what Bob knows about his resort. He'll take us through the snow-making operations and he'll tell us every detail about those machines—how much snow they make, what pressure is involved, how often they are used, you name it. Then we'll go over to the ski school and he'll know how many instructors he's got, what countries they are from, how many students pass through his resort each year. Then we'll go to the business offices and get the same detailed story. Bob knows his stuff. As a result, he's got a crackerjack staff who respects his knowledge and respects him as a leader. His resort has one of the highest percentages of resorts in North America of returning staff and of existing staff referring others to job openings. Deer Valley consistently ranks in the top three resorts in North America for best customer satisfaction by readers of *SKI* Magazine; in 2005, it was rated as the #1 overall resort in North America by *SKI* Magazine readers.

They have great confidence in their players.

In fact, they have greater confidence in their players' abilities than the players themselves have. Bill McCartney, former University of Colorado football coach and founder of Promise Keepers, said it simply enough: "Coaching is taking them someplace they don't believe they can get on their own."[7]

A better people leader sees potential in the individual and the team that they can't even see in themselves. A land developer can look

at a raw piece of land and see that if he added infrastructure and enhancements, he could change the market value of the resource. The better people leader sees similar long-term potential in her team members. To achieve this, a coach is entitled to be unreasonable—in a reasonable manner. A great example of this is my personal fitness trainer, Jodi. I've worked with her for years, and for most of that time I've considered her completely unreasonable in the things she's asked me to do, things I absolutely knew I did not have the capacity to do. But working with me step by step, she has continually managed to get me to a new level of fitness beyond whatever my previous capacity has been.

The better people leader does the same. She motivates, inspires, empowers, and leads her team to greatness, and she does not allow team members to substitute excuses for improvement.

They coach their players where they need it.

Legendary UCLA basketball coach John Wooden, known as the "Wizard of Westwood," coached his team to nineteen conference championships and ten national championships. With a record like that (and he had many more records under his belt before he retired), you might imagine he had some pretty slick coaching techniques— and he did. One of his most famous was a little trick he picked up while coaching high school ball: teach them how to put on their socks.

Coach Wooden found early in his career that if he could help his players prevent blisters, he could get more out of them. So one of the first things he did with his teams was teach them how to properly put on their socks, smooth out all the wrinkles around the toes and heel, and determine the right size of shoes.[8]

The better people leader knows the point of need for each individual on his team and works with the individual from that starting point. In Coach Wooden's case, if blisters were the need, then he

had his players put down the basketball and put on the socks—properly. He coached them at the point of their need even if the need seemed to have nothing to do with the game.

They know when to cheer and when to challenge.

My wife takes tennis lessons. She often comes home from a lesson and raves about her coach. In her mind, he is the best tennis coach in the state. I have no doubt that he is very capable, but the best in the state? Why does my wife feel so strongly about her coach? Because he knows when to cheer and when to challenge. She could do fifteen lousy serves in a row, and he still cheers her on. He will gush over the things she did just right, and then he'll appropriately point out ways she can make her next serve better. And what will she do? She'll hit that ball fifteen more times. It's not a matter of faking the positive or ignoring the problems. It's a matter of keeping the balance.

Constant criticism is a terrible people motivator. Constant cheering might seem a little Pollyanna. But better people leaders know when to cheer and when to challenge—and how to keep the balance appropriately tipped. I wish I could explain exactly how this is done. It is most certainly done on an individual basis—some people will need the balance tipped a little more to the "cheer" side, while others will do well with constructive challenges.

I knew of a young lady studying piano at a university. This particular woman was rather sensitive about her skill level because she had only started playing the piano in high school, whereas most of her classmates had played since they were children. She constantly felt behind the curve despite her obvious talent. At the university, she started with a piano teacher who was supportive and encouraging yet demanding and unyielding. The balance worked well for this young woman. She needed it tipped to "cheer," and her teacher understood that. However, after a year her teacher went on sabbatical and this

young lady was forced to start with another piano professor. She soon discovered her new teacher preferred fear and berating to motivate her students. Her new teacher would constantly tell her how terribly she played, how poor she must be at practicing, that she was lazy and didn't work hard enough, and how she would never be an accomplished pianist. The poor thing buckled under the constant barrage of criticism. She developed stomach ulcers and clinical depression, and she almost dropped out of her program. Fortunately, a new teacher joined the staff and teaching assignments were rearranged. This young woman went on to thrive under a new teacher and completed her music degree.

A better people leader knows, even if just through an attuned sensibility for her employees, when to cheer and when to challenge and the appropriate ways to do both. They publicly cheer and privately criticize. And they get the most from the people they lead in terms of productivity and loyalty.

They are patient, persistent, prodding.

The better people leader is in it for the long haul. Change, improvement, training, and reaching goals all require time, effort, and focus. From the better people leader, that requires patience, persistence, and prodding—of his team and of himself. Coach Wooden again is a good example of this principle. He began his coaching career in 1932 at a high school and moved on to UCLA in 1948. Guess when he won his first national championship? More than thirty years after he started coaching—in 1964.[9]

"If you want good things to happen, work for it," Wooden once said in an interview. "Know that you can't stand still. You've got to continue to improve. I don't think anyone stops improving. I hope I was a better coach my last year coaching than I was the year before. But I know full well in the earlier years there was more improvement

needed, and I improved more in the earlier years. But I never lost the fact that I must continue to improve. Never be satisfied. Always look for ways to be better."[10]

They minimize uncertainty.

Someone recently told me about a place at which she used to work that illustrates this point well, in the converse. It was a large corporation and she was an early-career employee in one of its many departments. The head of her department had become known for sitting in his corner office and scheming up ways to make improvements to the department. Shortly after she started working there, she saw a disconcerting pattern. Every few months the employees were called into last-minute meetings and were given new and seemingly random directives. In one particularly dramatic meeting, a slide was flashed for all to see (a slide that none had seen prior to the meeting), outlining a new organizational chart with everyone's new assignments, effective immediately. High-level managers who had been with the company for twenty-five years were spun off to non-managerial slots before everyone's eyes. As a result, the department was thrown into a tailspin. Tension skyrocketed, productivity plummeted, and unscheduled meetings were dreaded. The young employee told me that the actions of her department head proved to her that no matter what time and loyalty she gave, she would always feel uncertain of her present and future with the company. As a result, she left.

The better people leader does everything in her power to minimize uncertainty. In sports, the rules do not change midgame. They don't even change midseason. And when they do change, there is much discussion and expectation for the coming rule changes. Players never step on a field of play uncertain of the rules. The better people leader doesn't expect that of her players either. A business is dynamic and in constant motion. It is therefore the responsibility of

the better people leader to minimize wherever she can the uncertainty her team feels, and prepare them wherever she can for the uncertainty that can't be controlled. Most importantly, she needs to make sure her actions don't unnecessarily cause uncertainty.

To do this, she minimizes uncertainty wherever she finds it. If someone has a question about the direction of the company or concerns about the latest rumor, the better people leader answers it. The cost of not answering questions is the perpetuation of uncertainty, which leads to fear, which leads to paralysis. No one does their best work in a state of fear.

The better people leader also insulates her team from the vagueness of changing management initiatives. When the better people leader establishes goals, correctly prioritizes scorecards, and consistently coaches to those priorities, she not only reduces uncertainty but also instills confidence in her team members.

They are consistent.

The better people leader consistently coaches. One of the best tools for managing uncertainty—and one of the most desirable traits in a better people leader—is consistency. This doesn't mean she can't be flexible, quick-thinking, or open to change. It means she's predictable in her attitudes and trustworthy in her actions.

For my colleague and friend Bob Stauth, who served as chairman and CEO of Fleming Companies, Inc., consistency in leadership is synonymous with integrity. He described it to me like this: "Integrity says to others, 'Can I trust him? Is he consistent in his thought processes? Does he have a different response depending on who he's talking to?' " The better people leader demonstrates integrity through consistency in action, speech, and attitude.

SELF-ASSESSMENT

Now think about yourself. Coach Wooden liked to say, "It's what we learn after we think we know it all that really counts."[11] As I listed the above attributes, I purposely talked about the better people leader in the third person since I can't assume I'm describing you. Perhaps I am, or maybe I am describing the person you hope to become. Only you know how many of these attributes describe you today and how many will describe you in the future.

So take a few minutes to assess. First, make these attributes more real to you. I gave several examples of people who demonstrate these attributes; now think of examples from your life. Think of those in your life you would consider better people leaders. What attributes do they possess from this list? Do they have other attributes not on the list that you admire? On the pages provided at the end of this chapter, make a list of these people and then for each person, note the specific attribute and a specific experience that demonstrates the attribute in action.

Next, think of yourself. What attributes do you know you already possess? Make a list. What attributes do you think you possess, but would like to strengthen? Make another list. What attributes do you know you don't possess and need to focus on? Make a third list.

Keep these lists where you will see them often, and use them to set goals. Set a goal right now. Choose one thing from your want-to-strengthen list or your need-to-focus-on list and decide on something you can do immediately to improve that attribute in yourself. Do you need to cheer more than you challenge? Can you offer five people some positive feedback every day this week? Do you need to be better at learning your players' needs and coaching to meet them? Can you identify the needs of one player and think of one way to meet them at their point of need this week? Do you need to subordinate your own ego and focus on team excellence? Can you iden-

SELF-ASSESSMENT STEPS

1. **Make the Better People Leader attributes more real to you.** Think of those in your life you would consider better people leaders. What attributes do they possess from this list? Do they have other attributes not on the list that you admire?

2. **Think of yourself.** Make a list of the attributes you know you already possess. Make a list of the attributes you think you possess, but would like to strengthen. Make a list of the attributes you know you don't possess and need to focus on.

3. **Keep these lists where you will see them often, and use them to set goals.** Set a goal right now. Choose one thing from your want-to-strengthen list or your need-to-focus-on list and decide on something you can do immediately to improve that attribute in yourself.

4. **Make the Platinum Pledge:** "I will coach my team better than I am being coached."

tify a recent situation in which you may have focused more on yourself than your team? How can you do better next time?

See the global vision of becoming a card-carrying better people leader, and then start with digestible chunks to get you there. Be patient with yourself, but persistent and prodding at the same time, as you constantly seek improvement. And most of all, have confidence in yourself and your ability to lead people better. If you can do all that for yourself, chances are strong that you can do it for your team.

Finally, make the Platinum Pledge: "I will coach my team better than I am being coached." That pledge will mean different things to different people. If you are already working under an exceptional better people leader, then the bar is high for you. You need to lead your people more than exceptionally. If you are working under a less-than-exceptional leader, you are still required to give better than you get when it comes to coaching and leading. It's your chance to do better for yourself and your team.

THE HEART OF THE MATTER

Better people leaders exhibit similar traits. They:

- Have a global vision
- Can break down the vision into steps
- Focus on team excellence rather than their ego
- Know their team members
- Care about their team members
- Know their stuff
- Have great confidence in their players
- Coach players where they need it
- Know when to cheer and when to challenge
- Are patient, persistent, prodding
- Minimize uncertainty
- Are consistent

Assess yourself to find out what traits you already have and what traits you should be cultivating.

Traits of better people leaders I know:

Traits I have:

Traits to strengthen:

Traits to develop:

•three•

Get People Better

I once read about a young school teacher in Hawaii who taught fifth and sixth graders. In her very first class of students, she had a boy who spent most of his time out of the classroom with special education teachers. During the few hours he spent in her classroom each day, he was very disruptive and difficult to handle.

This teacher was in a tough spot. She had a responsibility to all her students, and this particular student made her job challenging. She probably had lots of choices on how to handle the situation, but she decided on a course of action that placed a great deal of responsibility on everyone in her classroom. Rather than having the problem removed or just gritting her teeth until the school year ended, the teacher decided to engage her students in a campaign to help

"Jimmy" get better. She asked them—when Jimmy wasn't in the room—to include him in their recess games, to sit with him at lunch, and to stop teasing and laughing when Jimmy acted out. Everyone agreed, and the experiment began.

At first Jimmy was shocked and suspicious of his classmates' behavior. But as they continued to treat him with respect and friendship, he gradually warmed up to them and his own behavior began to change. Over the course of the school year, the difference became marked. He improved both socially and academically. Even the school psychologist was surprised by the improvement in his test scores in a few short months. By the end of the school year, the boy who had been in special education since kindergarten had proven himself able to be a productive member of a mainstream classroom. He eventually stopped special education classes and went on to succeed in junior high school and high school—all because a teacher and fellow students decided to help him "get better."[1]

"Getting people better" is every manager's challenge—and opportunity. Have you ever heard (or said!) something like, "If only I could get better people, we'd be more productive around here." Or how about, "I shouldn't have to hold their hands while they do their job." These sentiments come from what I call the lazy manager mentality. If only they could get better people. If only their people knew what they were doing. If only they weren't burdened by the people they manage. If only, if only.

If only the manager's mentality were different. The better people leader doesn't wish away weaknesses on her team. She proactively approaches them and takes personal responsibility in her team's current performance and future growth. You might hear her say things like, "I am ultimately responsible for the performance of this team," or "What can I do to help you do your job better?" This is the proactive—and accountable—manager mentality.

The truth of the matter is, you have all kinds of power to get better people and to get people better. The individuals on your team each have strengths and weaknesses, and if you take the proactive and accountable approach to leadership, you will find you have the power to draw out their strengths, strengthen their weaknesses, and help them improve. You have the power to help them be successful.

But before I create any illusions, let me be clear: there is no magic formula; it will take thought, effort, and hard work on your part. It is much easier to wish for better people than to get people better. It may mean stretching beyond your own comfort zone, making very difficult decisions, and creating more work for yourself. But ultimately, getting people better will lighten your load and increase the success of your team. Here's the not-so-magic formula: (1) hire better than you have, (2) cut out the cancer, and (3) coach who you keep.

HIRE BETTER THAN YOU HAVE

You can read this two ways: *hire people who are better than the people you have* or *hire better than you have been hiring*. Both interpretations are accurate.

Hire people who are better than the people you have.

Let the best of the best in your company set the bar for who gets hired next. If you were to graph your current employees, you'd probably get something like a bell curve.

You'd probably have a fairly normal distribution of talent: some superstars, some non-superstars, and a bunch of folks in the middle who get the job done. Now divide that graph into quarters and you've set your benchmark. Only consider applicants who compare favorably with the top quartile of your bell curve. Eliminate the bottom seventy-five percent early in the process.

You can do this as a gut estimation—"I really like Sally, so I want more Sallys on the team." But you also need to carefully study that top twenty-five percent to understand what makes them the standouts. Analyze and then document the attributes that put those employees at the top. Are they aggressive sellers? Are they well liked by their peers? Do they have specific education or degrees? Are they full of ideas and energy? Are they hard workers who get the job done every time? Are they particularly bright in their fields?

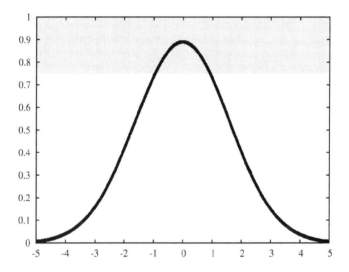

Come up with a thorough list, and it will help you with the next step of *hiring better than you have been hiring*. Think back to Shackleton's careful selection of his crew. He knew exactly what he was looking for—and he knew the importance of choosing the right *kind of person*, not just the one with the best skills or most experience. If you have a clearer picture of the kind of person you are looking for,

not just the *skill set* you are looking for, you'll be several steps ahead when it comes to knowing the right people when you see them.

Because you can't coach height—you have to recruit it. I once heard from a successful grocer that he hired entry-level employees based on how fast they walked past his store front. He said "pace" is difficult to teach. I've talked to others who believe "work ethic," unless instilled at a very early age, is a difficult attribute to develop later in life. Other attributes that can be difficult to teach might include "outgoing" or "people person" or "detail oriented." These are part of a person's "hardwiring." If these are critical to the position being filled, then identifying them and making them a priority in the talent search and selection process is imperative.

Hire better than you have been hiring.

Once you know what you are looking for, do a better job of finding it. There are many excellent books and Web sites out there to teach you techniques of recruiting and interviewing. Check out the resource section of this book for a short list of resources I have found particularly helpful.

In addition to the insights you can glean from these sources, I have my own list of techniques I have consistently found to be most helpful in doing a better job of hiring quality people.

Cast your net wider. It's never acceptable to bring in a warm body just to get the position filled. If you feel you have reached that point of desperation, you need to cast your net a little wider or think a little harder about the position you're trying to fill.

For Deer Valley Ski Resort, getting the best ski instructors is a critical part of their business. So rather than relying solely on the ski bum population that loiters around resort areas, they have cast their net farther afield. They have daily employee buses that run back and

forth to the major cities nearby. They also have purchased worker visas and actively recruit from Europe and South America.

Think creatively about the skills and experience needed for the position. At the Game of Work, we have a staff of salespeople who are vital to our business. It's not often that I have candidates who have done the exact kind of sales work I need done. But I have found that a variety of work backgrounds and experience can translate into a successful salesperson. For instance, one of the most important elements of a sales position in my company is the ability to comfortably and respectfully engage a CEO and his or her gatekeepers. So I will look for translatable experience. Maybe it's high-end real estate sales or financial planning experience. If you truly understand the jobs you are hiring for, you will be able to identify the *right* kind of experience, even if it isn't the *same* kind of experience.

You can also consider changing the rules if that will help you attract better players. JetBlue Airlines has done this with its reservation crew. The company has established a system for reservation agents so they can work from home. By doing so, they created a flexible situation that in turn casts a wider net.[2]

Over-interview. Several years ago we brought on a very senior executive to join our team. We had interviewed, checked his references, and done everything but call his mom to make sure we had the best guy for the job. Or so we thought.

As his tenure progressed, it became painfully obvious that he wasn't the guy for the job or for our company. We decided he needed to go, and we found ourselves in the middle of a lengthy and expensive battle. When the trauma was over and we were heaving sighs of relief, my assistant said to me, "I knew we never should have hired him. I could tell from the start he was not good for our company."

What?! She knew from the start? "Why didn't you say something?" I said. "Because no one asked," she replied matter-of-factly.

Over-interview the candidate. Let everyone meet him and let everyone weigh in, even if you don't think some people are relevant to the new hire. What did my assistant have to do with someone else on the executive team? In reality, very little. But she had enough to do with everyone at the company that it would have made sense to have her talk to him and have her offer her thoughts and feedback *before* we hired him.

In his book *Swim with the Sharks without Being Eaten Alive*, Harvey Makay recommends being creative with the interview process. His company's ten-step hiring process includes talking to candidates on the phone, visiting them in their homes, and socializing with them at a symphony or on a golf course. Makay's summary of the process is this: "If it sounds as slow and as painful as the Chinese water torture, imagine your pain at the other end if you have to fire someone you mistakenly hired. Then the investment doesn't look so bad."[3]

Test and profile. There are certain jobs you wouldn't think of hiring for without a test. Editors almost always face some sort of editing test to prove their skills and knowledge of the language. Other jobs require current licensure, such as nurses, doctors, lawyers, and contractors. Many jobs require portfolios or some other proof of the candidate's skills. I definitely recommend using some sort of test to ensure your candidates have the skills they claim to have.

I also highly recommend personality profiling. There are lots of good tests out there to help you understand how a potential candidate thinks and functions. These tests shouldn't be the only criteria for hiring someone, but they can offer a great deal of insight during the process. Check out the resource section for some excellent profiling instruments to consider using.

Call references. This might seem a little old fashioned to some, but boy can you learn a lot by talking to a few "outside" people about the person you are considering. I was working with a large corporation during the hiring of a senior vice president, and they decided to hire a woman based on her excellent résumé and positive interviews. But they decided to pass on calling references. Big mistake. After they brought her on, they soon realized that she could get the job done—as long as they didn't care about the body count. Napoleon in Stilettos, she came to be called. It was a long fifteen months that could have been averted if they had called a few references.

Checking references doesn't necessarily mean calling the people on the list of references given to you by the candidate. Proactively sniff out your own references. Do you know someone at a company where the candidate used to work? Do you know other people in the industry who might know him? Do you have an employment application that includes phone numbers of past supervisors? It's helpful to get an independent evaluation as often as possible.

Interview with scorecards. I was on a plane once, and the guy next to me pulled out a complex spreadsheet. He had seven pages with about thirty lines and fifteen columns on each page. He began poring over this spreadsheet, and with my penchant for scorekeeping and tracking, I just had to ask him what he did for a living. "I'm a scout for the NFL," he told me. "What do you focus on?" I asked. "I scout wide receivers in eleven western states," he said.

One position, one part of the country, and more than two hundred names were on his spreadsheet. The grid included information from football stats to academic stats to emotional health. Then the scout told me they start tracking these kids when they are freshmen in high school. When it comes time for the draft, they have eight years of history for every stat of every player they are considering.

It's not likely you will have been tracking your next set of applicants for the past eight years, but it better be likely that you will know exactly which stats you want to pay attention to. This goes back to the list you made from the top twenty-five percent of your employees. You should also use your current team goals, the score-cards you use to keep track of employees' performances, and your corporate mission statement for comparison and questioning during the interviewing process.

CUT OUT THE CANCER

I was working with an aerospace company that contracted with an Air Force base, and I was in a meeting with managers from various departments who were discussing a problem employee. Apparently this employee had been in one of the manager's departments and had been transferred to another manager's department. The second manager was having all kinds of trouble with this employee and was complaining about her to the group. The first manager nodded knowingly and said, "Yeah, she did the same thing in our department. She is a real problem."

The second manager asked incredulously, "Then why did you give her an outstanding rating?" The first manager's response: "That was the only way I could get rid of her."

While there are many things you can do to help an employee succeed, there are also times where the best thing for you and your company is to let that employee go work for the competition.

When the diagnosis is cancer, how long does the doctor wait to begin treatment? Does he wait a week? Does he wait a month? Does he say, "Let's put it on ninety days probation and do a review to see if it has improved?" Not likely. In fact, if the diagnosis is for someone you love, you wouldn't stand for a "ninety-day probation

period." You would demand a second opinion. You would switch doctors. You would camp out in the doctor's office.

The reality is, if cancer is the diagnosis, the treatment is immediate and aggressive. Specialists get involved; there are blood tests, x-rays, surgeries; and you and your doctors would do everything in your power to rid the body of anything even resembling a cancer cell. Once the problem is clear, the solution must be precise, immediate, and decisive.

There is a series of questions I often ask groups, and the responses are inevitably the same: "How many of you have ever discharged an employee?" Most people raise their hands. Then I ask, "How many of you have ever discharged an employee too soon?" I get a few raised hands and some quizzical looks. Then I ask, "How many of you have discharged an employee too late?" I get a lot of smiles and nods. Point made. When an employee becomes a serious enough problem that he needs to be terminated, you can't do it too soon, but you can do it too late.

What is a "serious enough problem"? Is it poor performance? Is it a bad attitude? Are others experiencing a drop in productivity or is the bad attitude rubbing off? Is it a blatant violation of corporate policy or even something illegal? You have to figure out what the cancer looks like in order to determine the best treatment. If someone on your staff is starting to slip, there may be hope to stop the decline and save the relationship. But if you can see that they have slipped beyond reach, then termination may be your next best step.

You also need to look closely at the margin to make sure you got the entire problem. Our Napoleon in Stilettos had brought in several of her cronies, and when the company terminated her, they had to look very closely at the swat team she had established. We found that several of the people she brought on also had to go. But

we also discovered that some of the people she brought on were capable and performed well without her influence.

I don't want to overstate this step in getting people better. I'm not talking slash-and-burn or bloodbaths. But I'm not talking hearts and flowers either. As a better people leader you sometimes have very difficult decisions to make, and if it means ridding your staff of a serious problem for the longevity and betterment of the rest of the team, then that's what it means.

COACH WHO YOU KEEP

This is where the rubber meets the road. You can't always hire and you can't always fire, but you can always coach.

I use the word "coach" very deliberately. People hate to be managed, but they love to be coached. When I think of being managed, I think of having little control, having no allowance to think for myself, and feeling unmotivated. When I think of being coached, I think of being encouraged, motivated, and empowered to do my job well and to get better at it.

I'll be honest with you, coaching is harder than managing. If you choose to simply manage your team, you could sit in your office for days at a time, create miles of spreadsheets, make endless assignments and reassignments, and be the sheriff for deadlines and corporate policy. Coaching, on the other hand, requires that you get on the field with the team—often. Coaching requires trust from both players and coaches. Coaching has to be regular, ongoing, and well planned. In short, coaching is a process and a mindset, not a spreadsheet or a deadline.

You should consider the rest of the book as the better people leader's guide to coaching who you keep. That's really what it is. I'll start here with a few of the big fundamentals around which to build your process and mindset as you go forward.

IMPROVE THE AVERAGE

As a better people leader, one of the first things you should do with any team is evaluate and establish the level of performance you will tolerate from each individual on the team. As my friend and colleague Bob Stauth points out, "Nothing de-motivates the stars like tolerance for the mediocre! You aren't doing anyone a favor when you allow them to perform at an 'average' level, and the top performers will hold your unwillingness to address these average performers as a weakness in *you*."[4]

I would even take it a step further. The only coaching immorality is keeping someone on your team whom you are unwilling to coach. You are doing your average employees no favors by tolerating "average." Think of the employee who has been with your company for fifteen years just plugging away at being average. What if, after putting up with his average performance for fifteen years, a manager decides to let him go? At age fifty, this employee may have few options. It didn't help him to be left at "average" for fifteen years, and I'm sure it didn't help the team to get only average work from him for fifteen years. It's a no-win situation when you let average slide by.

Something else to think about: someone who is average in one setting might be a superstar in another. By allowing someone to be average, you may be denying him the opportunity for success elsewhere. A better people leader *knows* the individuals she leads and tailors her coaching to the individual. She knows if the job someone is doing does not play to his strengths and what other opportunities might.

Here's an example: There was a midcareer production and plant manager who was "too hard on people" and couldn't get his team to embrace and support initiatives for improvement in their area. We had worked with him in two different locations, each time coaching him on his behaviors and setting goals for improvement.

But each time he seemed to "revert to type." Then the senior management team did a thorough review of his talents and abilities, and they decided to shift him to a logistics and transportation position where his responsibilities would be more focused on products rather than people. He is still flourishing in that position today and continuing to make positive contributions to the corporation. His leaders didn't accept an average people manager, and in turn they got an excellent logistics and transportation employee.

MEET THEM AT THEIR POINT OF NEED

You're going to get tired of hearing this: You need to know each team member so you know what their needs are. Here is a list of information you should know for each of your employees:

1. Name of employee's spouse or significant other.
2. Ages and first names of children.
3. What does he/she like to do off the job?
 a. List three favorite nonwork activities.
 b. What is his/her level of performance in each of these areas?
 c. What awards or special recognition has the person received?
4. Name one thing each of his/her children is good at.
5. What does the employee think his/her next position in the company will be?
 a. In his/her mind, how soon will he/she be ready to accept it?
 b. How closely does this agree with your assessment?
6. What would he/she do if the company went out of business?
7. Where does this person like to invest money?
8. What are this person's three greatest fears?

If you know the answers to all these questions, you have a solid foundation from which to build. Most importantly, you will be able to identify the employee's point of need. Does she need more training in order to do her current job better or to be qualified for a future job? Does she need to earn more money because of personal responsibilities? Is she starting to languish in her current job and need a new challenge or a new opportunity? Knowing your team members allows you to know their points of need, and that allows you to determine their next best step.

DETERMINE THE NEXT BEST STEP

Pat Summitt is the head coach of the University of Tennessee Lady Volunteers and the NCAA's all-time winningest coach.[5] In her book *Reaching for the Summit*, she talks about a natural phenomenon among her players (and I would add, among any workers): falling into a rut. Summitt is always looking for the next best step for her players, to get them out of their comfort zones and onto developing their game. I like her example of Mary Ostrowski.

> *Mary was a player with great fundamentals, but she wasn't aggressive about shooting the ball. She was passive. If she was standing right under the basket, she would still look to pass the ball. In December of 1983, we were in a tight game against Long Beach State. As the clock ticked down we designed a play to give Mary an open shot from the free throw line. When she caught the ball, rather than take the open jumper, she hit her teammate Lynne Collins in the back with a pass, which resulted in a turnover. We lost that game.*
>
> *I decided I would force her to shoot. I threatened. I cajoled. I made her run sprints every time she passed off. In the end, I made it a requirement that she take at least ten shots a game.*

She finished her senior year with a 17.8 points-per-game average, and she set an NCAA Final Four semifinal game record with a 31-point performance. We finished runner up two days later, losing to Southern Cal in the title game, but Mary made the NCAA All Final Four team.[6]

Pat Summitt knew her player's point of need—to become aggressive at shooting the ball—and she determined the next best step—*force* her to shoot. Summitt could have taken a different approach. She could have decided to accept Mary's average shooting ability. Instead, she took the next best step toward making Mary a better shooter. As a result, Mary had personal victories, including a record-setting game and making the All Final Four team. And the team gained a high scorer while keeping a player who excelled in other fundamentals.

For a player on your team, the next best step could be coming in on time, meeting deadlines she consistently misses, taking a leadership role on a project, or getting more training in her area of responsibility.

ESTABLISH A PLAYER DEVELOPMENT PLAN

A player development plan is an excellent way to determine and document what the next best steps are for an individual. Just like Pat Summitt, better people leaders employ a talent-development mentality. To coach people effectively, you must be concerned about more than just the task at hand—the thing due tomorrow or next week or next month. You need to look forward to the development of the player in addition to getting the immediate job done. You say to your player, let's get you better at the job you are doing today and let's prepare you for the next job you want.

The way to do that is four straightforward steps:

- **Keep:** These are the things the player is doing just right. Full steam ahead on these things.

- **Accelerate:** These are the things your player does well but could be doing better, faster, more of. Pick up the pace in these areas.
- **Start:** These are the things your player isn't doing but should be. Start.
- **Stop:** These are the things your player is doing but shouldn't be. Stop. Immediately.

PLAYER DEVELOPMENT PLAN

NAME: _____ COACH:_____

Behavior to:	Fill Current Assignment	Qualify for Next Level
KEEP		
ACCELERATE		
START		
STOP		

I have included an example of a chart I developed to track each player's development. I recommend charting for a player's current position as well as charting in preparation for the next position. And the player should see and use the chart. These player development plans aren't your secret notes on your team members. They are important individualized road maps that each player should discuss

PLAYER DEVELOPMENT PLAN

NAME: CJ **COACH:** CHUCK

Behavior to:	Fill Current Assignment	Qualify for Next Level
KEEP	Complete routine daily tasks: timely cash deposits, A/R, A/P Oversee payroll completed by outsourced payroll company	Oversee subordinates to assure timely reporting, collections, reducd days outstanding A/R Oversee investment accounts and ROI
ACCELERATE	Look for and complete cost reduction and analysis projects Begin looking for tasks to be delegated to others	Improve skill set with classes in specific financial areas Research and selection of financial software and training Research vehicles for increasing investment ROI
START	Become more involved in and understand cash flow forecasting Find or hire part-time employee to assume non-financial duties in your current area of responsibility	Provide analysis and recommendation to CEO/COO of financial and strategic tactics to improve profitability Report to CEO/COO on improved strategies for cash and investment management
STOP	Stop tasks that are non-financial in nature and delegate to replacement or new hire	Replace tasks that can be done by a lower-cost employee with those with a higher ROI in financial areas of cost reduction, profit improvement

with you and use to guide their progress.

I will leave this topic with a blank plan from which to model your own player development plans as well as one I filled out for one of my own employees to help you see how it can work. And by the way, with the help of multiple player development plans over the years, this employee went from an entry-level position to CFO through additional training, night school, introduction to computers and software, and additional advanced education in financial and investment strategy. He now oversees daily operations, payroll, taxes, pension planning, HR and investment securities, and real estate.

THE HEART OF THE MATTER

"Getting people better" is every manager's challenge—and opportunity. The better people leader doesn't wish away weaknesses on her team. She proactively approaches them and takes personal responsibility for her team's current performance and future growth. The individuals on your team each have strengths and weaknesses, and if you take the proactive and accountable approach to leadership, you will find you have the power to draw out their strengths, strengthen their weaknesses, and help them get better. These are the practical ways to do that:

- Hire better than you have.
- Cut out the cancer.
- Coach who you keep.

·four·

Why People Don't Do
What You Ask

Here's a coaching dilemma for you: You have a good person who isn't doing good work. You know he is skilled and talented and could be contributing better than he is. But he isn't. Why not?

When it comes down to it, there are only four reasons people don't do what you ask them to do:

- They can't
- They won't
- They don't know how
- They don't know what you want

Once you've identified the reason, there are steps you can take to coach them in the right direction—for their own success and the success of your entire team.

THEY CAN'T

Some people simply cannot do the task they've been asked to do. They don't have the skills. They don't have the aptitude. They don't have the license. Whatever it is, they simply cannot do it. If someone asked me to perform surgery, I would have to say, "I can't." If someone asked me to be her lawyer, I'd have to say, "I can't." If someone asked me to build a database, I'd have to say, "I can't." I don't have the qualifications, training, or skill set. I simply cannot do it.

Of course, you probably would know before you hired me to perform surgery whether I had been to medical school. But there are times when one of your team members truly cannot do a task or perform a duty you ask of him, when you anticipated that he could. When that happens, you have options.

One option is to reassign him. Realistically assess what he *can* do and what roles need to be filled on your team, and make a better match. For example, you may have asked someone to lead a project team when, let's face it, he can't. He is really a better software developer than a project leader. Keep him on the team as the lead engineer but find someone else to lead the overall project. You don't want to lose his skills altogether if it is simply a problem of a good worker doing the wrong work.

Sometimes you will want to lose his skills altogether. If he simply cannot perform the job functions he was hired to perform, then you need to replace him. "Cut out the cancer" comes into play, and you need to re-evaluate. Did this person end up in the position of "can't" because of a promotion or misassignment on your part? Then you need to know the individuals on your team better than you do. Or was he erroneously brought on in the first place because of a poor job description or a poor interviewing process? Then hire better than you have been hiring. Make sure you aren't bringing on people who

can't do the whole job for which they are being hired because of flaws in your own process or criteria.

THEY WON'T

Maybe they're stubborn. Maybe they're rebellious. Maybe they're lazy. Maybe they don't feel like it. Whatever the reason employees won't do what they are asked, it all boils down to motivation. They are not sufficiently motivated to act. We would hope that a strong personal work ethic would be motivation enough to give 110 percent every day on the job, but it's not. I would be out of a job if that were the case. I have built the Game of Work around the observation that people are more motivated to act in certain situations and less motivated to act in other situations. That motivation can be harnessed and channeled to get people to reach for their personal best on the job as well as in other areas.

Motivation is a reason for action. The more in tune you are with the motives of your employees—the reasons they feel inclined to act—then the wider the opportunities to motivate them. It gets back to *knowing* your employees.

The key, then, is to tailor the motivator. You may tailor it to an entire group of employees to reach group goals, or you may tailor it to each individual to reach individual goals. You should really do both. And how do you know what motivates your employees? Well, you can use all kinds of techniques to learn their motivators—from profiling to observation to eavesdropping. The most effective way is to simply ask them: "Here is what I want you to accomplish. What can I do to help you move forward in the most productive manner?"

You might be surprised what you learn when you ask. In some environments, people will be startled at just being given the opportunity to express themselves. No one has ever asked before. Knowing

that you are willing to listen to and act on their thoughts and ideas will probably be a motivator in itself.

As your team members share their individual motivators, you'll probably get a wide range of responses. You may learn that Joan has worked many long hours on her project and would appreciate a free Friday off. That could be a reward for her efforts. Tim wants to go back to school part time and needs a more flexible schedule. Perhaps a more flexible schedule could be a reward for reaching his performance goals. Mary has expressed a desire to grow in the company. Maybe you can reward her with extra training or with an assignment on a project she would find interesting. And John wants to take his family on a big vacation next year, so maybe the chance to earn a performance-based bonus is exactly the motivation he needs to step up to the plate and knock it out of the park.

I have to acknowledge here that, although it is rare, you will come across people who simply have a bad attitude. They won't because they won't. They aren't interested in being motivated and there is little you can do, no matter how you try to tailor the motivator, to make them want to do what they are asked to do. Mike is a classic example of "won't." He was hired as a manager at a manufacturing facility and was energetic and enthusiastic about the job. But then he was transferred. He was moved to a less cosmopolitan part of the country, and to be honest, he wasn't happy about it. He also did not appreciate his new boss. The man was rather autocratic and didn't care much for the whole idea of "team player." Mike's response to his new circumstances was "won't." He refused to respond to the requirements of his job or to engage with the team to the point of severe disciplinary action. In the end, he persisted with an independent mindset that bordered on insubordination. The company had no choice but to fire him.

Mike was later hired by a company that was a Game of Work client. The job requirements were essentially the same, but the boss and the environment were very different. At this company, Mike's motivation and enthusiasm were rekindled and he became a top performer here.

The lesson learned is twofold: in some situations a player cannot be motivated; in other situations, the problem lies with the coach, not the player.

THEY DON'T KNOW HOW

"They don't know how" is different from "they can't" in a fundamental way: They *could learn how* if they were trained. Imagine me in an operating room. I suppose I could eventually learn how to replace a knee or bypass an artery. But it wouldn't be very cost-effective for an employer to have me undergo that kind of training. However, you certainly can imagine scenarios where someone on your team is perfectly capable of taking on a responsibility if she is trained to do it.

Maybe it is something straightforward that a little software training will take care of. You need a database built and maintained, so you send someone to learn Access. Maybe it is something more involved and less defined. You want someone to take on affiliate marketing responsibilities but she has more experience with branding. So you have her work alongside your other affiliate marketers, send her to conferences, get trade magazine subscriptions for her, have her buy some books. She is capable, but she doesn't know how. So you train her.

To make sure she gets the right training, do some fundamental assessing to determine what kind of training she will need. Assess her basic skills and develop a list of augmentations needed, then prioritize the list. With a prioritized list, you can develop a reasonable

sequence of training as well as a timeline for when you want her up to speed. As the coach, you should work with her individually and demonstrate the skills you are asking of her. If you don't have those skills yourself, refer her out for training from people who do. Then follow up regularly to make sure the training you needed to happen was achieved.

We once hired an intern to join our sales staff who we thought had some excellent qualifications. Burke was a business school student and an Olympic-level athlete. He was full of excitement about our company and was anxious to learn all he could about the Game of Work. He clearly wanted to succeed at his job.

So we gave Burke all the training he would need. We taught him how to use the phones, how to use the script, how to interact appropriately to engage CEOs and their gatekeepers, how to seal the deal. We gave him all the tools he needed. And on his first day on the phones, he didn't make a single call.

His supervisor asked if anything was unclear or if there was anything else that could be done to assist him. Burke told him no, there was nothing else he needed. He confessed that he just didn't feel comfortable talking to CEOs. He didn't have the confidence to do it.

In this case, his supervisor had to step beyond teaching the responsibilities of the job and had to coach the person. Burke's point of need was self-confidence. His supervisor worked on this by offering more encouragement and reassurance that Burke did truly have capability to engage potential clients. The supervisor clearly defined the quantity and quality of work expected and mapped out an acceptable level of growth over the term of the internship. His supervisor also helped Burke better understand the principles of the Game of Work so that he understood why the CEO was the right person to approach.

With all this coaching, Burke was able to gain the confidence he lacked and have a successful internship. He also took his experience with him to his next internship. It was with a large multinational corporation, and he was named Intern of the Year at this company. Burke credited the coaching he received working with us.

THEY DON'T KNOW WHAT YOU WANT THEM TO DO

"What" is the easiest problem to solve. It is possible that someone isn't doing what you want her to do because she doesn't know what you want her to do. How clearly was the expectation communicated? Could she repeat back to you what you want her to do? Was anything left "understood" but unspoken?

"What" is solved through clearly defined goals, well-designed and executed scorecards, and thorough player development plans. Don't be afraid to target the lowest common denominator as you define goals and design scorecards for the whole team. This doesn't mean you treat your team like kindergarteners. But it does mean you should err on the side of too clear rather than not quite clear enough when it comes to explaining what it is you want accomplished.

A note of caution as you think through these reasons in relation to your team: You can mess this up in a variety of permutations. You can fire someone who needs to be trained. You can train someone who needs to be motivated. You can give goals to someone who needs to be fired. Be careful to diagnose before you prescribe. It will save you backpedaling and frustration. It's the old adage: "Measure twice, cut once."

THE POWER OF WHY

Let me mention two other ways you can help a good employee do good work. First is the power of *why*. When you understand and are addressing the reasons people are not performing as you

would like them to, you free yourself and your team to move to the next level of productivity and motivation. I call it the "have to" versus "want to" environment.

In a "have to" environment, a worker takes on a victim mentality. "I have to be at work by 8 a.m." "I have to create monthly reports for my boss." "I have to make fifteen cold calls every day." I have to do this or that and I have no choice. I am a victim of my company's policies.

Inevitably there is some level of "have to" in every job. Yes, there are requirements, and you "have to" do them. But too often managers leave it at that. "You have to do it, so that should be reason enough to sit there and type up your report." We can do more to create a "want to" environment. We do it by how we talk to each other. Every time we ask someone to do something, they have three questions: Why do you want that done? When do you want that done? How do you want that done?

The question people want answered the least is *how*. I hate to be told *how*. It insults my intelligence. When you tell me *how*, you are saying I'm not smart enough to figure it out on my own. But if I've *paid* for the how or *asked* for the how, I'm all over it. If I've hired a ski instructor or an accountant or a personal trainer, I'm all over it. But an unsolicited *how* is an affront to my intelligence.

Why is what we like to be told most. We love to know why. We love it because we like to understand context. Knowing *what* we need to do and knowing *how* we need to do it doesn't give us context. It gives us instructions. But knowing *why* we need to do something helps us understand the bigger picture. It helps us understand why our task or our role helps accomplish the bigger picture. We feel like contributors rather than cogs.

We also love to be told why because we know what it means— it means we're one of the important people. To the important people

we insist on explaining *why*. To the unimportant people we simply tell *how* or *what*. Are our team members important enough to merit a *why*? Or do they merely merit a *how*?

Everyone on your team is important enough to merit a *why*. The U.S. Department of Labor reports that the primary reason people leave their jobs is because they feel under-appreciated.[1] A Careerbuilder.com survey reports similar findings with forty-three percent of workers saying they do not feel valued by their employers.[2] Something as simple as including them in the discussions of why something needs to be accomplished or why something needs to change can have a significant impact on employee motivation and acceptance of responsibilities. A simple discussion of why will have a significant impact on your team and will prompt a powerful shift from "have to" to "want to."

COMMON SENSE

The other way to help good employees do good work is through common sense. We use the term "common sense" all the time, as if there is some common level of sensibility that somehow we should all be tapped into. A person has common sense if he or she does what you would do in the same circumstances. That's how people usually feel. But the reality is, "common sense" isn't very common. We all have different backgrounds, experiences, levels of education, personal beliefs, and values. You'll find there are few things that can be truly considered universally "common" sense.

So common sense isn't something we innately come with, but it is something that can be learned and taught. You create common sense, common passion, common attitudes, common culture among your team. The definition of "common sense" is just that, "common" sense—commonly agreed-upon sense, commonly agreed-upon principles and philosophies.

Let me explain and wrap up with an example. The Ritz-Carlton Hotel Company is known worldwide for its level of customer service. I can assure you its level of customer service is no accident. That reputation has grown out of a very deliberate corporate cultivation of common sense. Each new employee is given a minimum of 310 hours of training in the first year of employment and is assigned a departmental trainer to ensure they understand the skills, knowledge, and standards necessary to successfully complete the job.[3] Then employees are given more than one hundred hours of customer service training annually after their first year to keep them firmly grounded in The Ritz-Carlton way.[4] Employees memorize and internalize a set of Gold Standards that includes the corporate credo, a motto, Three Steps of Service, the Service Values, and the Employee Promise. In the Gold Standards you'll read things like "The Ritz-Carlton is a place where the genuine care and comfort of our guests is our highest mission"; "I am always responsive to the expressed and unexpressed wishes and needs of our guests"; and "By applying the principles of trust, honesty, respect, integrity and commitment, we nurture and maximize talent to the benefit of each individual and the company."[5] All of these statements are designed to build "common sense" among Ritz-Carlton employees.

These principles, understood and internalized by each Ritz employee, set the standard for their entire way of thinking. The Ritz-Carlton definition for common sense in customer service is not an abstract they hope their employees come with. It's a concrete they spend millions of dollars each year teaching and cultivating.

And within the very detailed expectation of *what* and *how*, the Ritz has also included an explicit *why*: "We are ladies and gentlemen serving ladies and gentlemen."[6]

As a result, the Ritz-Carlton has been showered with customer service praise. It has been ranked number one in luxury hotels by

Consumer Reports and J. D. Power & Associates. It has been named the best business hotel chain by *Forbes* magazine. It has received the people's choice award for the luxury and upscale hotel categories in *Travel Weekly.* And the Ritz-Carlton Hotel Company is the first and only hotel company honored with the Malcolm Baldrige National Quality Award from the United States Department of Commerce. It is also the only service company to receive the award twice.[7]

THE HEART OF THE MATTER

There are four reasons people don't do what you ask them to do:

- They can't
- They won't
- They don't know how
- They don't know what

Once you've identified the reason, there are steps you can take to coach them in the right direction: (1) using the power of "why" and (2) cultivating common sense. People feel empowered when they understand why they are asked to do something. It helps them move from feeling like they have to to feeling like they want to. Knowing why can help you create "common sense" for your team—a set of commonly agreed upon values, principles, and philosophies that can be taught and learned for the success of the entire team.

·five·

Scorekeeping for Success

One of your most valuable tools as a better people leader is your scorekeeping system. Correctly designed scorecards build common sense, explain why, provide motivation, and make very clear the *what* in what's expected of your team. Most importantly, scorecards give your employees a way to succeed—a way to win.

George Odiorne, the father of management by objectives, said, "If you can't measure it, you can't manage it." I take it a step further: if you *don't* measure it, you can't manage it. Keeping score is a way of measuring, but with some fundamental differences. I like to "keep score" rather than "measure" for a very specific reason: everyone loves to score and everyone hates to be measured. By its very nature, scoring is positive, exciting, and cause for celebration; being measured is negative, nerve-wracking, and cause for concern. Scoring is also proactive: it's something the employee does for herself, something

she has control over. Measuring is passive: it's something done to the employee by someone else, something she has little or no control over. So while measurement is important, keeping score is a better way to do it. Let's go over the basics of scorekeeping.

Scorekeeping must be objective and relevant.

You either made a basket or you didn't. You either produced one hundred cans of soup per minute or you didn't. You either went thirty days without an on-the-job accident or you didn't. You either closed five deals this week or you didn't. Scorekeeping is objective. It is not based on someone's opinion or their tastes or their preferences. Scorekeeping is a quantifiable measurement of an accomplishment. A basket is a basket, even if someone on the team thought it should have been a dunk instead of a layup. It's an objective measurement.

It is also relevant. Years ago I started working with what was then a small grocery store chain. Their primary measurement of success was net profits for each store as a whole. It's certainly an important thing to look at. But figuring out how to increase those net profits based on such a general measurement was tricky. So we decided to introduce a more relevant scorekeeping system. We introduced scorecards for each department in the store. Each department manager—meat, bakery, produce, etc.—was responsible for keeping track on a daily basis of her department's contribution to the store's overall net profits. With the new scorekeeping system, store management and department managers had a much clearer picture of how the overall net profit was achieved and each department's role in it. This allowed them to identify strong points and weak points and address them accordingly. The system also allowed them to objectively and quantifiably track the success of promotions and campaigns department by department. And the system was perfectly relevant to the bigger goal: increase overall store profits.

Scorekeeping must be self-administered.

Scorekeeping works best when it is self-administered. Some managers make the mistake of doing all the scorekeeping themselves, or having their assistants do all the scorekeeping. All this does is delay the game. If a manager or her assistant keeps score, then it could be days, weeks, or heaven forbid, a year before the player knows the score. Remember the painful and ineffective annual review? If scorekeeping is self-administered, then all players know exactly what their score is at any given time; they know if they are winning or losing; and they know what they need to do to improve their score. Make scorecards self-administered and every player will know his score.

Make scorecards self-administered and people will also trust them. People trust what they can see and touch. When folks keep their own score, they are not skeptical of the data source. They know exactly where the data came from and how it got on their scorecard. That trust is an important element in motivating future action.

Scorekeeping must offer a comparison.

Scorekeeping should compare current personal performance, past personal performance, and an accepted standard. The emphasis is on personal. Golf would no longer be a favorite national pastime if everyone who plays golf had to compare their own performance to Tiger Woods or Annika Sorenstam. Rather, golf allows every individual to set his own bar and mark improvements based on his own past and current performance. The accepted standard is par. If your personal performance doesn't equal par, you still get to judge yourself on your own performance by determining your handicap. It's an objective system that allows every player to know where he is, how far he's come, and what the standard is.

You can guess how this works in a business setting. When workers self-administer their own scorekeeping, they know how they

did last week, they know how they did last month, they know how they are doing today. The accepted standards are the overall goals of the team. A player can look at the overall goals and look at his scorecards in comparison and know exactly where he stands with himself and with the accepted standard.

At the grocery store chain, there was a manager in the meat department who got very excited about the idea of scorekeeping. As he kept score, he saw that his department averaged about $100,000 per week in revenue. In his enthusiasm, he set a major goal for his department. He decided one year that his department would do $250,000 the week after the New Year holiday—a week well known to be the slowest of the year. He knew his past performance, he knew the standard, and he knew with a good action plan he could beat both. The store manager, while also excited about scorekeeping, thought the meat manager was setting his sights too high. But nothing was going to stop him and his team. And nothing did. He involved his entire department in the race for the record. They stepped up their list of specials and in-store demonstrations, increased sampling, and greeted every single customer as if that person was the most important customer the store had. That week they made $255,000. Which leads to the last point about scorekeeping.

Scorekeeping must be dynamic.

Players know the score during the game, so they can change their behavior in order to win before time runs out. I can assure you this meat manager knew every day, perhaps every hour, how close his department was to reaching its goal for that banner week.

It is critical that a scorekeeping system is dynamic—it is updated and changing during the game so players know the score at any given time. Think about the way gymnastics or figure skating is scored. The gymnast doesn't know the score until he's completed his

THE BASICS OF SCOREKEEPING

Scorekeeping must be objective and relevant.
Scorekeeping must be self-administered.
Scorekeeping must offer a comparison.
Scorekeeping must be dynamic.

routine. Of course he does his best during the routine, but he has no way of making adjustments or improvements during the routine based on the score. It's the old annual review method: tell the player the score after the performance is over. But in basketball, a player knows with every basket whether he is winning or losing, and you and the player have the opportunity midgame to change the performance. I'm not speaking negatively about gymnastics, but when it comes to scorekeeping in a business setting, we're looking at the Lakers rather than the U.S. gymnastic team (although business leaders can learn a lot from gymnastics about hard work, perseverance, and excelling). A good scorekeeping system will allow you and your players to check the score regularly and often, and will allow everyone to track the progress and make improvements while there's still time on the clock.

Let me reiterate: A well-designed scorekeeping system builds common sense, explains why, provides motivation, and makes very clear the *what* in what's expected of your team. Most importantly, scorecards give your employees a way to win.

You'll notice I haven't said too much about goals. Goals are the foundation of almost every business philosophy out there. I'm in

complete agreement. In recreation, the goals are clearly defined. They need to be clearly defined in business, too. If they are not, we are forced to concentrate on activity and ultimately become enslaved by it. Have you ever seen someone who seems busy all the time but never seems to accomplish anything? Without a goal or an objective, what does activity lead to? Not much!

But here's the twist we've seen work time and time again in the real world: scorekeeping must precede goal setting. You need a score-keeping system before you can determine goals. For the grocery store chain, the original goal was to increase overall store net profits. It's certainly a worthy goal, but with no way of knowing how those net profits were obtained in the first place or of tracking the score, the goal was pretty hollow. We had to let go of the big goal for a bit and backtrack. We established department-by-department scorekeeping systems. Then we understood where the strengths and weaknesses were. Did they need to increase their sales per customer? Did they need to increase the percentage of store customers who made a purchase in a given department?

With a clearer vision for each department, we were able to determine department goals. Then we were able to determine a store goal. With a relevant, objective, dynamic scorekeeping system, we were able to get buy-in from each department head. They didn't feel they could control the overall store profits, but they did feel they could impact their own department's net profits. We had buy-in because we had a scorekeeping system. There was a basis for the goals and a way to achieve them—a way to win.

The most important thing a good scorekeeping system does for you is provide the basis for appropriate feedback. One of the most important principles of being a better people leader is providing appropriate feedback. To provide appropriate feedback, you've got to have benchmarks and some kind of accounting system to know if

you are ahead or behind. That's what scorecards do for you. The primary reason for scorekeeping is to allow coach and player to agree on when, what type, and how much feedback is appropriate.

THE HEART OF THE MATTER

One of your most valuable tools as a better people leader is your scorekeeping system. Scorekeeping doesn't have to be elaborate, but it has to be done right. Here are the fundamentals:

- Scorekeeping must be objective and relevant
- Scorekeeping must be self-administered
- Scorekeeping must offer a comparison between current personal performance, past personal performance, and an accepted standard
- Scorekeeping must be dynamic

The most important thing a good scorekeeping system does is provide the basis for appropriate feedback. To provide appropriate feedback, you've got to have benchmarks and some kind of accounting system to know if you are ahead or behind. That's what scorecards do for you.

·SIX·

Appropriate Feedback

The book *How Full Is Your Bucket?*, by Tom Rath and Donald O. Clifton, starts with a study done of one thousand American prisoners of war who had been held by North Korea during the Korean War. The overall death rate in the North Korean POW camps was a staggering 38 percent, but the captors rarely used physical punishment and torture on the prisoners. These prisoners weren't physically beaten to death. They were mentally beaten to death.

The primary method was feedback—deliberately selected feedback. The captors had four major tactics. First, they rewarded prisoners for informing or snitching on other prisoners. Next, they made prisoners confess to each other bad things they had done or good things they had not done. Then they withheld any positive emotional support, such as uplifting letters from home, while they piled on negative support, such as letters from home mentioning

overdue bills or deaths. Finally, they worked daily to undermine loyalties to each other, to leadership, and to country so prisoners believed it was "every man for himself."

The interesting thing about these tactics is how passive they were. If the captors had beaten the prisoners, the prisoners would have had something to fight against. But by giving them bad news from home or making them share their regrets, there was nothing to incite a defense mechanism. The consequences were devastating. Prisoners literally gave up and died.[1]

Sadly, I shared this account with a client once, and her response to me was, "That sounds like my company."

Feedback is a daily nutrient. If you don't think feedback is important, try counting the number of mirrors in your house, try ignoring your wife when she asks how she looks, try ignoring your child when he wants to show you what he made at school, and try ignoring your dog when you get home from work. The ability to deliver appropriate feedback is the most important human relations skill you can develop. By contrast, the delivery of inappropriate feedback is the world's biggest morale killer.

Too often the feedback is inappropriate. It usually comes in only two varieties: negative and nonexistent. As the POW camps demonstrated, both varieties are destructive. Ironically, the third variety—appropriate—can be the most constructive and positive tool in the better people leader's tool belt. It's Newton's Third Law: for every action there is an equal and opposite reaction. If negative feedback can be so powerful, then positive and appropriate feedback must be just as powerful. I would take it a step further and say positive and appropriate feedback is more powerful.

WHY PLAYERS DON'T ASK FOR IT AND COACHES DON'T GIVE IT

So if appropriate feedback is so important, and your six-year-old will jump up and down until you stop and look at his picture and then proudly hang it on the fridge, why don't workers jump up and down? And why don't managers stop and look at the picture?

We'll start with the workers. Players often don't ask for feedback because they didn't care for the response they got last time. Maybe they were ignored. Maybe they were brushed off with a quick, "Yeah, yeah, that was fine," response. Maybe they opened the floodgates and got all the feedback you had bottled up for months. If they didn't get appropriate feedback the last time, they will be once bitten, twice shy the next time.

Asking for feedback has also become a sign of weakness. People who are always asking for feedback are sometimes considered needy or insecure or just a pain. If your players think that asking for feedback will brand them a problem worker, they will learn not to ask for it.

And sometimes they won't ask for it because they don't think they need it: no news is good news. If negative feedback is all they are used to, they count it as positive not to be getting any feedback. "There must not be anything wrong with what I'm doing because nobody has said anything."

On the coaches' side of things, they have their own list of reasons for not giving feedback. Probably one of the biggest is that it takes time and energy. If your six-year-old is jumping up and down to show you a picture and all you want to do is dump your briefcase and ditch your tie, it's an effort to stop, smile, ooh and ahh, and find an empty magnet on the fridge. It's the same at work. If you are too busy doing "other stuff," you don't have time to run around to each desk and comment on the work everyone is doing. You may also have

the "no news is good news" mentality. If I don't stop by your desk today, you must be doing fine.

But here's the rub: if something is important enough to ask someone to do, it is by definition important enough to give feedback on. If you learn how to do it right, feedback will not be a negative experience or a sign of weakness; rather, giving appropriate feedback can become one of your most valuable tools for getting people better.

REINFORCE BEHAVIOR WE WANT REPEATED

Reinforce behavior we want repeated. Think about how this works. Whether you are a parent with a child, a manager with an employee, or a spouse with a spouse, if someone does something you don't like, you are quick to respond to it. "Get back in your bed! It's past your bedtime!" "You came in late this morning. You need to get here on time." "You never pick up your socks!" We identify and respond to behavior we *don't* want repeated and too often we give that kind of behavior all the attention and all the feedback.

If you go to a bank, what are the behaviors you want in your teller? You want accuracy, speed, and politeness. But if you looked at how banks track tellers' performances, you wouldn't find gold stars rewarding them for being polite or for balancing to the penny. The reports you would find are generally called "overages and shorts." Banks track what tellers do wrong, not what they do right.

A better approach is to reinforce behavior we *do* want repeated. What do you do to make bedtime special for your child? Have you ever said thank you to an employee who came in early to get extra work done? Do you thank your spouse for making the bed or mowing the lawn? How can a bank reward or recognize tellers who do balance to the penny every day for a month?

Few do it better than the people at SeaWorld. When training animals, they only focus on what is done right. SeaWorld animal

ambassador Julie Scardina was interviewed by *USA Today* and asked about the techniques SeaWorld uses to train its animals. I thought her responses were insightful: "We work hard to create an environment that is interesting, fun, and stimulating and draws attention to behavior we want repeated. We pay attention to good behavior; don't make a big issue if a mistake is made. . . . The furthest we go is neutral. Not giving them any attention is an effective type of discipline. We find that fear of discipline has a dampening effect that can lead to defensiveness or aggression. . . . We use a system that does not put trainers at odds with the animals, but constantly reinforces the positive relationship."[2]

If only we all had or were bosses like the SeaWorld trainers. But most of us operate in a system that tracks problems more than successes. In industries where safety is an issue, there is a measurement you'll often see: the AFR, or Accident Frequency Rate. It's the number of accidents reported per 200,000 man-hours worked. The AFR measures safety in a work environment by tracking how many times accidents happen in this time period.

Imagine if that were turned around. I worked with a large bottler in Alabama for quite some time. As a manufacturing facility, they kept close track of their AFR. For about a decade they tracked the number and for about a decade they had a goal of zero accidents. But for a decade they averaged twelve accidents per year. Try as they might—education campaigns, constant reminders, threats, and cajoling—they could not reduce the number of accidents. When we began working with them, we got our heads together and came up with a new scorecard. Rather than tracking how many accidents they had, we tracked how many hours they went *without* an accident.

What do you think happened? They had tried to reduce their AFR for ten years without success. But as soon as they started counting the hours they did not have an accident, the accidents went

down—way down. They went from averaging one accident a month to having twelve months without a single accident. Twelve months, zero accidents! A fellow named Jack Mitchell was the plant manager I worked with, and he explained it to me this way: "Nobody wanted to be the one who broke the record, so everybody thought about safety like they never had before."

Jack also had developed the habit of regularly going down to the production floor to check out the operations and look at the scorecards, which were prominently displayed. That's how he caught people doing their jobs right. He looked at their scorecards and acknowledged their good work, usually with something as simple as a sticky note left on their scorecards: "Great day, Bill. Keep up the good work." "Way to go, Steve. Huge improvement."

He had one employee who wasn't doing very well with his hours without an accident scorecard. Because the scorecards were all hung next to each other, this employee saw the sticky notes left on others' scorecards. The employee had apparently taken notice and was working to improve his record. The plant manager was on the floor one day and noticed that this employee had caught up and was doing well in his safety record. However, Jack wasn't doing sticky notes that day and just let it go.

Well, the employee wasn't having that. The employee marched up to Jack's office and called him on it: "Where is my sticky note? My record is better! I should get a note on my scorecard, too." Jack was tickled pink that the employee cared so much about getting a dumb little sticky note.

People love to be caught doing it right. How many times have you heard someone complain that if they mess up or make a mistake, they immediately get in trouble, but if they go for weeks doing everything right, no one cares? Think about that in terms of recreation. Have you ever been at a little league game where a run wasn't cheered

or a college football game where the stands went silent when a touch-down was made? What if fans said, "That's what they are supposed to be doing out there, so why should we cheer for them when they're just doing their jobs?" Why is it in work we are reluctant to pay special attention to someone who is doing it right, but in sports we go wild?

Some of the best and most appropriate feedback we can give our team members is to make a fuss when we catch someone doing their job right. It doesn't even have to be a big fuss. It can be a coach sticking her head in someone's cubical just to say, "Thanks so much for that report. It's exactly what I needed." As Mark Twain said, "I can live for two months on a good compliment."[3]

ALWAYS CELEBRATE BETTER

Several years ago in my company we had an incentive trip to Hawaii for those who had reached some major goals we set. When we were there, we went on a dinner cruise and our host blew the traditional conch shell horn to the sunset. We were all impressed and decided we needed a conch shell in our office, so we took one home with us. Have you ever tried to blow a conch shell? They aren't easy to get a sound out of, but when you do, there's no missing it. It just so happens that I can blow a conch shell. We determined to use the shell to celebrate better. Every time we got a signed contract with a down payment, I would be called upon to blow that shell. And when the shell blew, the crowds went wild. There was a mini celebration for every sale. Can you imagine what that did for morale and for sales? We didn't blow the shell every time a lead went cold or every time a company said no. We drew attention to the successes, not the failures. Failures tend to draw attention to themselves.

At the Alabama bottler, they implemented a program of dinner on the company when certain performance goals were met. It wasn't a very expensive celebration, but it was very effective. Workers

were allowed to bring their spouses or significant others, and the dinners were held as a group at a nice local restaurant. These small celebrations were incentive for the workers, but interestingly, they became incentives for the workers' spouses, too. The workers started getting pressure from home to make their performance goals because their spouses also looked forward to the dinners.

Always celebrate better. Don't deny your employees a little celebration, or a big one, for their successes. People trade their performance for your applause, your appreciation, your approval. Don't cheat them! If they work for you full time, they give you more than two thousand hours a year. How much feedback would we have to give before we were over the top? And how much better do your celebrations need to become before they are too good? Chances are you are a long way from going over the top with your celebrations. Most companies have lots of room to improve their celebrations before they hit the ridiculous mark.

I know of a department in a company that highly discourages team lunches (even when the team members pay for themselves) because it gives the appearance of not working hard enough when everyone gets up and leaves at the same time. In this department, they have two major deadlines each year, and the weeks leading up to the deadlines are frantic. By the time the deadlines are successfully met, every staff member feels cause for celebration. So do you know what these poor employees have done? They've taken to sneaking out of the office in small groups and meeting up at a nearby restaurant so they don't get in trouble for going to lunch together.

Think about what it would take for the coaches of this team to help them celebrate better. Change the unspoken rule about going to lunch. *Help* them plan a lunch outing after the deadlines have been met. If they wanted to really shock the employees, the coaches could pay for the lunch! Celebrating better could be that simple.

Another fellow I know started with a regional supermarket chain early in his career. In his position, the potential for a large bonus was a very motivating factor for him and most of his colleagues. After his first year, he qualified for his bonus and looked forward to the "big night"—a celebration of the year's successes and the acceptance of individual bonus checks. It was a celebration everyone looked forward to.

Except the CFO. The CFO wore a black armband to the awards ceremony and for the following week at the office. Although the gesture was meant to be humorous, as a young employee with the company, my friend wasn't quite sure how to take it. Was the company really struggling to give out bonuses? Unfortunately this act, done in jest, tainted what might have otherwise been an excellent celebration of the employees' accomplishments.

When my friend had been with the company for a few years and had risen up the ranks to the point of working more closely with the CFO, he recommended that the CFO pass on the armband at future awards ceremonies. He explained how the armband had made him feel as a new employee, and the CFO, who had never thought of it in those terms, ended the tradition. The "sign of grief" had provided a very powerful, unintended message of negative feedback during a time when it should have all been positive. And without the armband, they were able to celebrate better.

Most companies have room to celebrate better. It doesn't have to be dramatic or expensive—removing the armband didn't cost a penny! But it does have to be better. Think about your own team and their successes. How can you always celebrate better?

APPROPRIATE FEEDBACK ISN'T ALWAYS POSITIVE

Let's take a reality check. All this positive reinforcement and celebrating can sound Pollyanna-ish. Running a business or manag-

ing a department or leading a project is hard work and you may not consider yourself much of a party animal when there are major responsibilities to accomplish. Plus, there are plenty of times when the feedback needs to be negative, when there's nothing to celebrate, and when bad behavior needs to be stopped.

But that is also part of appropriate feedback. It is often appropriate to say, "I have noticed that you are short with customers, and that is not how we treat customers in our store," or "We haven't blown the conch shell once for you this month. We need to talk about how you are doing with your sales," or "You have had two safety incidents in the past six months and the average is zero. Why is that happening?" It goes back to the Player Development Plan: Start, Stop, Accelerate, Keep. There are things that need to be stopped and things that need to be stepped up, and your team members may never know what they are if you withhold appropriate feedback—even if that feedback has to be frank and not necessarily positive.

It also goes back to the only coaching immorality: the only immorality in coaching is being unwilling to coach someone on your team. If someone on your team needs appropriate feedback that isn't necessarily positive, it is unfair to them to withhold that feedback. In fact, the withholding of feedback is one of the most severe forms of psychological punishments we can inflict on one another. If you are going to be a productive coach and a member of your team needs correction or additional guidance, your responsibility is to give it to that person. Not giving negative feedback when it is needed can impede the development of your team members as much as not giving positive feedback when it is needed. When done kindly, objectively, and straightforwardly, even receiving negative feedback can be considered a positive experience by your team members.

IMPROVEMENT TEAMS

The better people leader not only needs to give appropriate feedback, but she also needs to create an environment in which players too can give appropriate feedback. I go back to the employee at the bottling plant who improved his safety record. The plant manager had created an environment in which that employee could give feedback to the manager: "I did a good job and I want my sticky note." It wasn't offensive or dismissed. It was feedback going both ways. The plant manager got the message, and he did a better job at catching this employee and others doing it right.

One of our clients is a carpet cleaning business. The owner of the business created a forum for feedback by implementing a daily early morning technicians' meeting that occasionally starts with donuts, but always ends with a discussion of procedures and results. In this meeting technicians get to provide feedback as much as the owner does. This meeting doesn't replace one-on-one time with the technicians, but it does provide an open forum for frank feedback. One of the company's major problems was redos—having to return to a customer's home or office to clean the carpets again. "Once we started talking about it and showing each other how we were doing, the number of redos decreased," the owner told me.

Another company I work with developed something they call "improvement teams." It is a pretty radical approach to getting feedback up and down the line, but it really works for this company. In this company there are two thousand people. The president and his administrative assistant hold a meeting every other week. The people at this meeting come from each of the twenty-five departments in the company and not one of them is a manager. They are informally selected by their peers to go to the meeting.

The rules of the meeting state that no subject is barred. In this meeting, employees can come and talk about what's getting in their

way of better serving the customer, or explain what additional resources are needed to meet customer expectations, or discuss something they are feeling unhappy or uncomfortable with. During the meeting, anything that can be resolved on the spot is resolved on the spot. If it cannot be resolved, the president takes it upon himself to work on a resolution before the next improvement teams meeting. Everything is recorded in the minutes and the minutes are distributed to everyone in the company.

By establishing to-the-point meetings designed just for feedback and improvement, you might be amazed at the information that is shared and the reinforcement that takes place. Think of the technicians sharing tricks with each other, which ultimately results in fewer redos. That is very helpful feedback for the technicians struggling to meet expectations. But it's also positive reinforcement for the technicians who are doing their jobs well. They get a chance to share their expertise and get positive reinforcement as a result: "That's a good idea. I hadn't thought about that," or "Thanks for the tip. I used it yesterday and it worked like a charm."

When establishing improvement team meetings for your team, there is one critical truth you need to take into account. When you go into a meeting, there will be people who want only to talk about the problems and there will be people who want only to get more attention for the successes. You cannot leave the meeting until you have discussed both. The tendency will be to spend the meeting on the problems and forget the successes. But the meeting can't end until you've acknowledged both. There are two reasons for this. One, you owe it to your team to acknowledge their successes. Second, if you overlook successes, you may be overlooking opportunities to learn from them. How were they achieved? How can we repeat that success in the next situation? Can the experience we've had with a success be applied to a problem we currently face?

THE HEART OF THE MATTER

The ability to deliver appropriate feedback is the most important human relations skill you can develop; it can be the most constructive and positive tool in the better people leader's tool belt. By contrast, inappropriate feedback, which can be either negative or nonexistent, is the world's biggest morale killer. To give appropriate feedback, first understand why players are usually reluctant to ask for feedback and why coaches tend to avoid giving it. Then you can begin to implement better methods for providing feedback, including reinforcing behaviors you want repeated, celebrating better, and forming improvement teams. You will even be better equipped to handle situations in which less-than-glowing feedback is appropriate.

·seven·

Honoring Your Mentors

Now let's take these concepts to a higher level. I'll illustrate with an experience I had not too long ago. I was in a meeting where I asked a group, "Who is your mentor?" I thought the response was interesting. Nobody hemmed and hawed trying to think of someone. It was a small group and I could see that the people got a little sparkle in their eyes as they immediately thought of a person they considered a mentor.

I asked around the room to find out more. One person's mentor was his father. Another's mentor was her first boss in her chosen profession. Another's was a college professor. Then I asked, "Why are they your mentors?" Again, the response was immediate. They all had reasons on the tips of their tongues. One earned the title by providing valuable support and advice through a lifetime of situations. One earned the title by taking the time to train and teach and give

individual feedback. One earned the title by pushing for more insights and new thoughts and perspectives.

As we went around the room and each person talked about his or her mentor, I could see not only that each person could have gone on and on had time permitted, but I could also strongly sense how much each person respected and cared about the mentor in his or her life. And perhaps even more importantly, they all made it clear how much they felt their mentors cared about them because of the time the mentors took with them individually.

While each had a different experience and a different reason for choosing his or her mentor, the mentors shared a common trait: they cared about the individual. It's that old saying again: they don't care how much you know until they know how much you care.

THE BEST OF THE BETTER PEOPLE LEADERS

In my estimation, becoming a mentor is becoming the best of the better people leaders. Not everyone can be a mentor. It takes a rather special individual. A mentor is a counselor and a guide—someone who teaches more than how to do a task, but also how to handle situations and make good decisions and live a productive life. Only the best of the better people leaders rise to the status of mentor. The evolution might look something like this: A manager tracks tasks, details, mistakes, and progress. A coach does all that is required to manage, but he also draws the very best from his people through motivation and feedback and proactive game plans. A mentor steps beyond coaching the team and focuses on coaching the individual. Coaching can be effectively accomplished one-on-many, but mentoring can only be one-on-one.

One-on-one is key. In past generations, mentoring was not only a standard practice, it was almost the only practice. For millen-

nia, knowledge was passed from father to son, mother to daughter, master to apprentice. Mentorship is how society progressed.

Mentorship seems to be experiencing something of a rebirth in today's society. You'll see mentors offered through community business programs like SCORE or the local SBA office. You'll find all kinds of articles and books about mentoring and being mentored in business or education. You can hire a mentor in the form of a life coach. Brigham Young University introduced an elaborate mentoring program to its campus community a few years ago. The school had the ongoing debate about whether or not it was commissioned to be a teaching university or a research university, but the proactive university president decided it could be both and introduced the concept of mentored learning. As a result, professors have been given the incentive to include students right down to the freshmen level in their research. Professors still have the opportunity to research and students have the opportunity to learn one-on-one from a master.

You'll also often hear of mentoring within companies as a way to train new employees or recently promoted employees in their new responsibilities. Like at the Ritz-Carlton, a more seasoned employee will be assigned to mentor the new employee, and it is her job to see that the new employee learns the ropes.

The beauty of true mentors is that they transcend the organization. You may have gained them by working at an organization— a boss, a colleague, a professor—but they can continue to act as a mentor and you can continue to consider them a mentor long after you or they leave the organization or your daily interactions stop.

In fact, I ask you the same question I asked the group in the meeting: "Who is your mentor?" I know someone instantly springs to mind. You may even have two or three people spring to mind. I'll bet you didn't instantly think of the organization that person came from. You definitely know, and can definitely say, "My mentor is Jane

Johnson. I met her while working at Acme." But I bet your very first thought was, "My mentor is Jane Johnson." The mentor transcended the place of introduction.

Finally, mentorship has to be organic. Rarely can mentors and mentees be assigned to each other. The relationship usually grows out of a natural affinity or connection. That's why not every boss/employee or father/son or professor/student relationship develops into a mentoring relationship. If you think about your own mentors, you'll agree that mentors are chosen, not assigned.

HONORING YOUR MENTOR

It's not enough just to know the person's name and have fond memories of whatever he taught you. You need to do more with that name. You now have a responsibility to repay that person's kindness, efforts, and wisdom. So let's do an exercise:

First, **think of the three most influential mentors you have known in your life and write their names on the pages provided.** If you don't have three, then write two or four or whatever is the right number for you.

Next, for each mentor, **list the three most powerful coaching attributes or skills each of them demonstrated.** What did they do for you? What did you learn from them? Why are they your mentors? What did you see in them that you have hoped to emulate in your own life and career?

Once you've done that, **prioritize your list based on importance.** What are the most important attributes or skills you learned from each person? Put your list in order of importance to you in your daily life.

Now I want you to spend some time with this list. **Review your list every day for a month.** Make it a point—every day—to remember what your mentors have done for you and have taught you.

And finally, **act to honor their memory.** The review of your list should lead to specific actions. Determine what you will do to honor all that your mentors have taught you. How will you treat your family or your colleagues or your employees or your neighbors differently based on what you learned from your mentors? Be specific. Write down thoughts and ideas and goals and specific actions. In thinking of a team member, you may want to refer back to the Player Development Plan discussed earlier. Look at key items on the employee's plan and think of how one of your mentors might work with that individual. Then act as if you were your mentor. The more you find situations to "act as if," the more your mentors' qualities will become a natural part of who you are.

And "act as if" is a tremendous way to give back. Becoming a better people leader is great, but to be the best of the better people leaders, you have to pay it forward. I hope by the end of this book you are doing a much better job of leading your people, getting your people to be better employees and better people. I hope you have learned skills and insights and tips and tricks to help you draw from your people their best efforts.

But to become a mentor yourself is to become the best of the better people leaders. That's how you honor your mentors. You do for someone else what they did for you. I learned this principle from one of my first mentors, Ferrell Lee Hunter. He was an executive vice president for a company and I worked at one of its franchises. He taught me how to sell services in my first commissioned sales position. One of the things I admired most about him was his cool head in hot situations. He had this incredible ability to get calmer the more agitated others became. He was a wonderful peacemaker.

Because of all he taught me about dealing with sales and dealing with people, I was in an almost constant state of effusive appreciation. Then on one occasion, as I was again trying to over-thank

him, he simply said to me, "It makes no sense to give it back to me. I already had it before I gave it to you." Then he added, "Don't give it back, give it away."

Of course it can't be a direct repayment like a bank loan. It has to be a "pay it forward" repayment. In honoring your mentor, you have to give it back or "give it away" to the next in line. It could be in a specific mentor relationship with someone coming up the ranks behind you. It could be in a mentor relationship with a niece or a nephew, with a kid from your neighborhood or your church, with a family friend. Or it could be working as a Big Brother or a Big Sister or donating your time to a community center for youth. There are lots of ways to become a mentor and pay it forward.

Bob Stauth decided to offer himself as a mentor to the MBA program at his local university. He was the CEO of a large corporation, and after his retirement, he spent seven years volunteering at the school. He started out mentoring students one on one. They could sign up to go to lunch with him and spend an hour talking, asking questions, and seeking advice. Then Bob met another retired CEO who was also interested in mentoring. So they decided to double team the students. One student could sign up for forty-five minutes with both former CEOs, and twice a week these old dogs would meet with bright-eyed students and have a grand old time.

"We were, to many, the only successful adults that they had any direct interface with in their entire lives," Bob told me. "It was a great way to give back."

PETE HARMAN

Let me tell you about another man I have considered a mentor. His name is Pete Harman, and he was the first franchisee for Kentucky Fried Chicken.[1] Pete owned a café in Salt Lake City called Harman's Café.[2] In the early 1950s he met Colonel Harland Sanders,

who at the time was peddling his secret recipe for fried chicken. The two struck up a business relationship and a friendship, and as a result of their meeting, Kentucky Fried Chicken was born and the way restaurants are franchised was changed forever.[3] Pete was Colonel Sanders's first franchisee and is credited with coming up with the name "Kentucky Fried Chicken," with the idea of a takeout chicken family dinner, and with the venerable "bucket of chicken."[4] Pete went on to own hundreds of KFC franchises in the western United States and the Colonel went on to make fast food history.

HONORING YOUR MENTOR

1. Think of the three most influential mentors you have known in your life and write down their names.

2. List the three most powerful coaching attributes or skills each of those mentors demonstrated.

3. Prioritize your list based on importance.

4. Review your list every day for a month.

5. Act to honor their memory.

While I completely admire Pete's business success, it's his success as a decent person that I really want to talk about. His right hand man for years, Jay Alexander, tells one story that gives real insight into the character of Mr. Harman. When Harman's Café first began selling

the Colonel's secret recipe fried chicken, it was as an additional item on a full café menu. But they wanted to give it a big promotional push, so they brought in their usual window painter to paint an advertisement on the café's windows promoting the fried chicken.

When the fellow was there to paint, he told Pete, "You've got to have a snappy name. You can't just call it fried chicken." So they talked about it and the painter came up with "Kentucky Fried Chicken." Pete agreed, saying that Kentucky was just far enough away from Utah to sound special. So they dubbed it Kentucky Fried Chicken and splashed it on the windows of the café.

Well, several years later, when the window painter was elderly and nearing the end of his life, Pete and his associate Jay Alexander went to visit him. Pete knew this fellow was struggling financially in his elder years, and he said to the guy during this visit, "Did you ever get any royalties for coming up with that name?" The fellow smiled and shook his head. So Pete matter-of-factly wrote out a check and handed it to the man and his wife. The old window painter choked up, and his wife openly wept.[5]

"I can sum up Pete Harman in four words," Jay said. "'Do the right thing.'"[6]

I first met Pete in 1985. We had just published the first edition of the book *The Game of Work*, and someone in the Harman Corporation saw it and thought they'd like to have us come out and do a presentation for their managers. So they contacted me and we talked and they ended the conversation by saying they would have to have me talk to Pete Harman before I would be allowed to address the managers.

Now, I didn't know anything about Pete at the time, and I will admit I was caught off guard and felt a tiny bit defensive that they had to pull in the big guns to make sure I was approved to talk to their managers. But I agreed and set up a meeting with Mr. Harman.

At that time, they had about three hundred KFC operations in the western United States, and in walked Pete Harman wearing an inexpensive blazer and trousers and plain shoes. He sat down with me and laid it out. "Chuck, I want you to understand that this is not about your qualifications or your ability," he said. "I just need you to understand, before you talk to this group, how very, very special these people are." Then he started to tell me their stories. He told me about his workers coming from nothing and moving up into management and opening new stores and getting the chance to buy into the chain. He told me about a hardworking couple from Oakland, California, who opened a KFC in Sacramento, and how the wife worked opening and closing shifts because her husband couldn't read well enough to open and close the tills each day. He told me story after story about his people, and he reiterated that I couldn't talk to them until I knew what kind of people I would be talking to—incredible people who were dear to Pete's heart. By the end of the two-and-a-half hour meeting, neither of us could hold back the tears.

To me, that's a better people leader. That's the best of the better people leaders. Pete Harman knew his people. He empowered them with opportunities to shine. He treated them fairly and honestly and with dignity. He praised their excellent work not just to their faces but also to a cowboy management consultant who would be hired to talk to them. He genuinely cared about his people, and they, in turn, genuinely cared about him.

I have tried to honor Pete's example ever since as I've led people and taught people to lead others in a way I hope would have made Pete proud. This book could be considered one of those "honoring" moments for Pete and Ferrell and other mentors I've had in my life. Think of your mentors, and immediately start paying it forward with whomever you are called to lead.

THE HEART OF THE MATTER

Becoming a mentor is becoming the best of the better people leaders. A mentor is a counselor and a guide—someone who teaches more than how to do a task, but also how to handle situations and make good decisions and live a productive life. It's not enough to have fond memories of whatever your mentor taught you. You have a responsibility to pay it forward. A simple exercise can help you get started:

1. Think of the three most influential mentors you have known in your life and write their names on the page provided.
2. List the three most powerful coaching attributes or skills each of them demonstrated.
3. Prioritize your list based on importance.
4. Review your list every day for a month.
5. Act to honor their memory.

Priority	Name of Mentor	Skills/Coaching Attributes

·eight·

It's the People

I want to bring it back to where we started. Even though this book has been about how to be a better people leader, by now you should be acutely aware of the central word in that phrase: "people." "People" comes before "leader." To evoke Sir Ernest Shackleton again, your ship cannot sail without its people. So if this book is about you, it is about teaching you how to do better for your people.

So what will you do when you put this book down and get back to your people? What attributes are you committed to developing or strengthening? How will you find the best people, weed out the worst people, and coach everyone you keep? How will you motivate, train, and assign your people so they can succeed in whatever they are asked to do? How will you cultivate common sense and use the power of "why" to strengthen your team? How will you design your scorekeeping system so your team has a way to win every day?

How will you improve your ability to give quality and appropriate feedback? How will you reward the behaviors you want repeated and how will you better celebrate your team members' successes? And how will you pay it forward to the next in line?

Think of Ernest Shackleton and how attuned he was to exactly which kind of people were right for his expedition. Think of Don Pritchard and his ability to learn the strengths and weaknesses of his team members and then play to their strengths. Think of Coach Wooden who met his team members at their point of need—right down to their socks. Think of Jack Mitchell who made getting a little yellow sticky note the highlight of his employees' day. Think of Bob Stauth who so appreciated what his own mentors had done for him that he decided to offer himself as a mentor to hundreds of MBA students.

I hope you have also thought of other better people leaders, the ones you know personally. Who are they and what have they taught you about doing right by your people? How will you pay forward their examples and influences?

As I said early on, becoming a better people leader is no simple task. Yes, there are some people naturally imbued with incredible attributes of leadership and they wield them well. But for most of us, it takes time, commitment, dedication, and perseverance to become a better people leader. But don't your people deserve that much from you? As their leader, you have the power to enable and ennoble them—or demoralize and crush them. They deserve to be enabled and ennobled. In return, they will do all that you ask of them and more, and tomorrow you will see both personal and team successes you cannot imagine today.

In his book *1776*, David McCullough captures a moment in the leadership of George Washington that embodies the power of a better people leader. It was December 31, 1776, the last day of the

year celebrated as the birth of a nation, but also a year of unprecedented violence and struggle. As the year drew to a close, the conflict was not won, but the army's enlistments were set to expire. On January 1, 1777, the soldiers were free to return to their homes.

I will pick up with McCullough's account:

> *The last day of 1776, [Washington] made a dramatic appeal to the veteran troops of the Continental Army to stay with him.*
>
> *Having no authority whatever to do so, he offered a bounty of ten dollars for all who would stay another six months after their enlistments expired that day—a considerable sum for men whose pay was six dollars a month. . . .*
>
> *One of the soldiers would remember his regiment being called into formation and His Excellency, astride a big horse, addressing them "in the most affectionate manner." The great majority of the men were New Englanders who had served longer than any and who had no illusions about what was being asked of them. Those willing to stay were asked to step forward. Drums rolled, but no one moved. Minutes passed. Then Washington "wheeled his horse about" and spoke again.*
>
> *"My brave fellows, you have done all that I asked you to do, and more than could be reasonably expected, but your country is at stake, your wives, your houses, and all that you hold dear. You have worn yourselves out with fatigues and hardships, but we know not how to spare you. If you will consent to stay one month longer, you will render that service to the cause of liberty, and to your country, which you can probably never do under any other circumstance."*
>
> *Again the drums sounded and this time the men began stepping forward. "God Almighty," wrote Nathanael Greene,*

"inclined their hearts to listen to the proposal and they engaged anew."

Before the day would end, Washington would learn that by vote of Congress he, in fact, had been given the authority to "use every endeavor," including bounties, "to prevail upon the troops . . . to stay with the army. . . ." Indeed, for a period of six months the Congress at Baltimore had made him a virtual dictator.

"Happy it is for this country," read part of the letter transmitting the resolution, "that the general of their forces can be entrusted with the most unlimited power, and neither personal security, liberty, nor property be in the least degree endangered thereby."[1]

Centuries later another American president, Ronald Reagan, summarized what Washington did for his troops and what you can do for yours: "A great leader is not necessarily one who does the greatest things. He is the one who gets the people to do the greatest things."[2]

That is your challenge. Focus on the greatness of your people and you will become great together.

Notes

CHAPTER 1

1. Margot Morrell and Stephanie Capparell. *Shackleton's Way* (New York: Viking, 2001), 209.

2. http://www.pearyhenson.org/northPole1909/bookintro4.html

3. http://www.south-pole.com/p0000052.htm

4. Caroline Alexander. *The Endurance* (New York: Alfred A. Knopf, 2000), 9.

5. Morrell and Capparell, *Shackleton's Way*, 61–62.

6. Alexander, *The Endurance*, 54; Morrell and Capparell, *Shackleton's Way*, 61.

7. Morrell and Capparell, *Shackleton's Way*, 63.

8. Alexander, *The Endurance*, 21–22; Morrell and Capparell, *Shackleton's Way*, 58–59.

9. Alexander, *The Endurance*, 15, 23.

10. Ibid., 28.

11. Ibid., 18, 25.

12. Ibid., 25–44.

13. Ibid., 44.

14. Morrell and Capparell, *Shackleton's Way*, 98.

15. Ibid., 99.

16. Alexander, *The Endurance*, 89.

17. Ibid., 121, 135, 141.

18. Ibid., 141.

19. Ibid., 143–153.

20. Ibid., 164–165.

21. Ibid., 107, 145, 149, 171–176.

22. Ibid., 182, 185.

23. Beau Riffenburgh. *With Scott to the Pole* (New York: Barnes & Noble Books, 2004), inside jacket.

24. Morrell and Capparell, *Shackleton's Way*, 56.

25. Jim Collins. *Good to Great* (New York: Harper Business, 2001), 13.

CHAPTER 2

1. David DuPree, "It's All about the Team for Krzyzewski," *USA Today*, August 7, 2006.

2. Jim Collins. *Good to Great* (New York: Harper Business, 2001), 39.

3. http://en.wikipedia.org/wiki/Charles_H._Percy

4. Charles A Coonradt. *Managing the Obvious* (Park City, UT: The Game of Work, 1994), 171–172.

5. http://en.wikipedia.org/wiki/Charles_H._Percy

6. Ken Follett. *On Wings of Eagles* (New York: New American Library, 1983), 74–76.

7. Charles A. Coonradt. "Coaching Makes the Difference" (lecture).

8. http://espn.go.com/page2/s/questions/wooden.html

9. http://uclabruins.cstv.com/sports/m-baskbl/spec-rel/ucla-wooden-page.html

10. http://www.coachwooden.com/ (video interview on home page, approx. 7:45 min. along)

11. http://www.brainyquote.com/quotes/authors/j/john_wooden.html

CHAPTER 3

1. Karen Case Ho-Ching, "The Experiment," *Ensign,* June 2006, 8–9.

2. https://jetblue.recruitmax.com/ENG/candidates/default.cfm?szCategory=job prfile&szOrderID=13311&szCandidateID=0&szSearchWords=&szReturnTo Search=1

3. Harvey B Makay. *Swim with the Sharks without Being Eaten Alive* (New York: HarperCollins, 1988), 185–187.

4. Bob Stauth, e-mail message to author, August 28, 2006.

5. http://utladyvols.cstv.com/sports/w-baskbl/spec-rel/081806aac.html

6. Pat Summitt. *Reach for the Summit* (New York: Broadway Books, 1998), 230.

CHAPTER 4

1. Tom Rath and Donald O. Clifton. *How Full Is Your Bucket* (New York: Gallup Press, 2004), 31.

2. http://www.careerbuilder.com/share/aboutus/pressreleasesdetail.aspx?siteid=c bpr&id=pr117&ed=12%2f31%2f2004&sd=5%2f5%2f2004&sc_cmp1=cb_p r117_&cbRecursionCnt=1&cbsid=3db1b727aca44fb4a393e4ecab31dae2210 882003-WZ-2

3. http://www.ritzcarlton.com/corporate/employment/faq.asp

4. http://www.ritzcarlton.com/corporate/press_room/kits/baldrige.html

5. http://www.ritzcarlton.com/corporate/about_us/gold_standards.asp

6. http://www.ritzcarlton.com/corporate/about_us/gold_standards.asp

7. http://www.ritzcarlton.com/corporate/about_us/awards.asp

CHAPTER 6

1. Tom Rath and Donald O. Clifton. *How Full Is Your Bucket* (New York: Gallup Press, 2004), 17–26.

2. Del Jones, "Training Workers the SeaWorld Way," *USA Today,* August 21, 2006.

3. http://www.quotedb.com/quotes/1086

CHAPTER 7

1. http://www.kfc.com/about/history.asp

2. http://www.bluemaumau.org/kentucky_fried_chickens_first_franchise, http://www.bluemaumau.org/kfcs_first_franchisee_part_2. (This is a two-part podcast with Jay Alexander.)

3. Ibid.

4. Ibid.; http://www.deseretnews.com/dn/print/1,1442,595057690,00.html

5. http://www.bluemaumau.org/kentucky_fried_chickens_first_franchise, http://www.bluemaumau.org/kfcs_first_franchisee_part_2.

6. Ibid.

CHAPTER 8

1. David McCullough. *1776* (New York: Simon & Schuster, 2005), 284–286.

2. Elizabeth Dole. *Hearts Touched with Fire* (New York: Carroll & Graf, 2004), 145.

Resources

BOOKS ABOUT HIRING

Dinteman, Walter Anthony. *Zero Defect Hiring: A Quick Guide to the Most Important Decisions Managers Have to Make.* San Francisco: Pfeiffer, Division of John Wiley & Sons, Inc. 2003.

Grensing, Lin. *Small Business Guide to Employee Selection.* Bellingham, WA: Self-Counsel Press. 1991.

Ennis, Sarah J. *The Manager's Pocket Guide to Interviewing and Hiring Top Performers.* Amherst, MA: HRD Press. 2003.

Rosenberg, DeAnne. *A Manager's Guide to Hiring the Best Person for Every Job.* New York: John Wiley & Sons Inc. 2000.

Still, Del J. *High Impact Hiring: How to Interview and Select Outstanding Employees.* Dana Point, CA: Management Development Systems. 2006.

BOOKS ABOUT SCOREKEEPING

Coonradt, Charles A. *Scorekeeping for Success*. Park City, UT: Game of Work LLC. 1998.

PROFILING INSTRUMENTS

Inscape Publishing Instrument Based Learning Systems, focusing on DiSC Personal Profiles and Team Profiles: www.inscapepublishing.com

HR Chally Predictive Assessment System: www.chally.com

Kolbe Indexes or Kolbe Pure Instinct System: www.kolbe.com

Index

Made in the USA
San Bernardino, CA
03 November 2013